THE STORY OF
DIETRICH BONHOEFFER

THE STORY OF
DIETRICH
BONHOEFFER

RADICAL INTEGRITY

Michael Van Dyke

BARBOUR BOOKS
An Imprint of Barbour Publishing, Inc.

Published by Barbour Books, an imprint of Barbour Publishing, Inc., P.O. Box 719, Uhrichsville, Ohio 44683, www.barbourbooks.com

Our mission is to publish and distribute inspirational products offering exceptional value and biblical encouragement to the masses.

Member of the
Evangelical Christian
Publishers Association

Printed in the United States of America.

Dedication

To Beth.
You show me every day what it means
to "live for others" in a Christlike way.
Thank you for your love.

prologue

April 5, 1943 — Berlin, Germany

He looked older than his thirty-seven years. Deep lines radiated out from his eyes and across his face. His blond, thinning hair barely covered the top of his head, even if he had combed it carefully. His shoulders slumped as if they were carrying a lead weight. Sweat beaded above his eyebrows.

During the last six months, Dietrich Bonhoeffer had been involved in two attempts to kill the leader of his country—a madman named Adolf Hitler. Both of those attempts had failed. Now, as he sat at a large oak desk in an upstairs bedroom of his parents' house, he painstakingly examined every document that was piled on the desk, looking for anything that might reveal his involvement in the plots against the Führer.

Thirty minutes earlier, he had phoned his brother-in-law, Hans von Dohnanyi, who was one of his fellow conspirators. When a man with a gruff voice answered the phone, Dietrich knew at that moment that Hans was in the hands of the Gestapo. The secret police force of the Nazi regime would be coming for him next.

As he went through the stack of papers, his mind raced. Should he tell his parents and sister, who were having tea in the kitchen below? Should he try to flee, and if so, where? All he knew for sure was that he needed to destroy anything that would help the Nazis convict him of treason. Thus he carefully examined each piece of paper and placed the ones whose contents looked dangerous in a circular steel wastebasket at his side. Several minutes later, he heard a knock on the front door downstairs and listened as his father shuffled across the floor to answer it.

In the mirror to his left, Dietrich could see himself, but he did not recognize the image. Gone were the robust muscularity of his youth and the smooth, round face that had always given him a boyish look. Now his youth lay on the other side of the time period represented by the papers on his desk.

When Dietrich looked at the last sheet of paper, his father, as if by divine signal, called him from the bottom of the stairs.

"Dietrich! Some men down here are asking for you."

Dietrich struck a match on the side of the wastebasket. "I'm coming," he called back. He dropped the match in among the papers. They slowly crackled into flame, and he watched until the last one had turned as black as tar. Then he calmly walked downstairs and gave each member of his family a brief hug before leaving with the men in dark coats.

He would never again see his parents as a free man.

They rode to Tegel prison in silence. The two men, who

had identified themselves as SS agents, had been almost cordial when they led him out to the black Mercedes. They were about the same age as Dietrich and perhaps had some lingering respect for his family's social position.

Dr. Karl Bonhoeffer, Dietrich's father, was one of the most respected psychiatrists in Germany. So esteemed was he that the Third Reich government had even asked him to evaluate certain "dangerous" prisoners, apparently so that the Nazis could know whether traitors to the regime were insane before they shot them. Dr. Bonhoeffer agreed to do the evaluations out of a sense of professional duty but not out of any sense of loyalty to the Nazis. He hated what the Nazis had done to his beloved Germany and how they had turned a great culture into a barbaric state.

Dietrich could not help thinking about his family as the car made its way toward the outskirts of Berlin. He thought of his older brother Klaus, who was also a part of the conspiracy and whose life would also be in danger. He thought of his brother-in-law Hans. Where could the Nazis have taken him, and what sort of abuse was he suffering? He thought of his sisters: Christine, who was Hans's wife; Sabine, Dietrich's twin and the one he could always confide in; and Susanne, the baby of the family, who was also the most free-spirited of the bunch.

And then he thought of his parents again, both in their seventies now, who had lost a son in the First World War and who were now in danger of losing two more. Though his father was an agnostic, and his mother did not go to church, Dietrich knew that they at least could rely on each other for strength. They were aristocrats from an ancient Prussian family. There was every reason to believe that they would be able to hold up under the strain, at least for a little while. Still, it pained him to be putting them through so much grief.

When they reached the prison, a bleak, concrete structure, Dietrich was led to a chamber where he was commanded to change into prison clothes. He asked if he could make a telephone call, but the officials simply ignored him. All of his personal belongings—watch, cuff links, wallet, and pen—were confiscated and placed in a small cloth bag. Then he was led along a corridor where all the doors were solid except for narrow slits where food could be passed through. One of these doors was opened, and Dietrich was pushed into a cell about ten feet long and six feet wide. Even in the dark, he could tell it was filthy.

In one corner of the cell was a small cot, and there was a tiny window above his eye level that let in a bit of late-day sun. Opposite the cot was an old stool. Dietrich placed it beneath the window and stepped up. He looked out and saw all of Berlin spread out before him. *Beautiful, doomed Berlin*, he thought. Though it was his home, and the place at the center of his dreams, he prayed for its defeat.

But only because that defeat would also mean the destruction of the Nazis.

Dietrich was kept in solitary confinement the first several weeks. His only exercise, which consisted of pacing back and forth in his cell, reassured him that he was alive, and also kept his legs from becoming stiff. The lights were dimmed from 8:00 in the evening until 6:00 in the morning, but Dietrich was never able to get more than six hours of untroubled sleep.

He was disturbed mostly by thoughts of what his imprisonment meant. What effect would it have on his recent engagement and marriage plans? Did it mean that his efforts in the resistance over the last two years were an absolute failure? Or could it possibly mean that this was the end of the world as he knew it? He tried not to let these questions dominate his thoughts.

On a less contemplative level, he was also deeply troubled by what he heard below him on the lower two floors of the prison complex. The constant sobbing and occasional screams of prisoners could be heard every night, as well as shouted curses.

As Dietrich lay on his thin cot, he tried to pray for these anguished men, but it was difficult. He had never seen them in the flesh. He did not know their stories. He did not know their crimes, if in fact they were criminals. ("Criminal" was just one more word whose meaning had been destabilized by Nazi propaganda. Criminals were now only those who impeded Nazi goals.)

Quickly, Dietrich realized that he would have to impose some sort of order on his new existence if he did not want to go crazy. Since his Bible had been returned to him, he resolved to begin reading it from beginning to end. He would also meditate on Scripture and pray at regular intervals throughout the day, like Daniel in the land of the Persians.

One day, Dietrich's cell door was opened by a young, blond-haired guard, who motioned for him to step out into the corridor. Dietrich left his Bible on the cot and obeyed.

"What is this?" Dietrich asked, not without fear, when he and the guard were standing together outside the cell.

"Orders have come down. You are to get half an hour of exercise in the yard every day."

"Oh, that is wonderful," Dietrich replied, pleasantly surprised.

11

The guard walked Dietrich down to the yard and then with him around the perimeter. Dietrich took the opportunity to look at some of the other prisoners in the yard. Most of them had faces that revealed more fright, bitterness, and brokenness than he felt himself. For a moment, he thought that this was a pretty good picture of what a world without God would look like. *Only an infinite amount of love could transform such an image,* he surmised.

Dietrich then turned to the guard and asked, "Am I such a dangerous prisoner that I need somebody continually at my side?"

The guard snorted in amusement, a gesture that surprised Dietrich. For some reason he expected all of the guards to be stone-faced.

"No, you are not dangerous," the young man replied. "The reason I, well. . .actually, I had something to ask you."

"Oh?"

"I heard that you will be moved to a larger cell tomorrow—"

But before he could go on, Dietrich quickly asked, "How did that happen?"

"Uh, I guess you have friends in high places," the guard said. "A General von Hase?"

A smile crept across Dietrich's face. "My uncle," he said.

"Yes, well," the guard continued, "this new cell will contain a desk and chair. So I just wanted to ask if you will need writing supplies."

Dietrich was speechless. He had been praying, but without much hope, for exactly that. His face gave the guard an affirmative reply.

"Will you need envelopes, too?" the guard continued.

12

And then before Dietrich could answer, he said, "Yes, I guess you will, of course."

"Th–that would be wonderful," Dietrich stammered.

The next day, Dietrich was moved into his new, more spacious cell. A few hours later, the guard arrived and gave him a pile of blank paper, several pens, and a few envelopes.

"I will make sure your letters get out, and there are more supplies when you run through these," the guard said. "Only one letter a week, though. At least at first."

"Thank you," Dietrich answered, barely able to contain a grin. "Thank you very much, uh. . ."

"Linke," the guard answered. "Corporal Linke. I just want to make sure that you have every comfort that is allowed."

And when Dietrich's eyes expressed surprise, Linke continued. "Germany may be fighting the Americans and the British, but you and I both know who our true enemy is. It is important for you to know that this is just a job to me, not a calling. I have a family to feed, and nonmilitary employment is hard to come by. Surely you understand?"

Dietrich nodded, and after Linke left he took a moment to send a prayer of gratitude heavenward for the unexpected blessing of a friend.

Before the light faded that afternoon, he sat down to write a letter to his family. It was his first letter as a prisoner of the Third Reich, and he worded it in such a way that it might encourage them about his condition.

Dear Parents,
*   I do want you to be quite sure that I'm all right.*
I'm sorry that I was not allowed to write to you
sooner. Strangely enough, the discomforts that one

*generally associates with prison life, the physical
hardships, hardly bother me at all. One can even
have enough to eat in the mornings with dry bread
(I get a variety of extras, too). The hard prison bed
does not worry me a bit, and one can get plenty of
sleep between 8 P.M. and 6 A.M. The only thing that
bothers me, or would bother me, is the thought that
you are being tormented by anxiety about me and
are not sleeping or eating properly. Forgive me for
causing you so much worry, but I think a hostile
fate is more to blame than I am.*[1]

Dietrich folded the letter, placed it in an envelope, and
blew out his small candle. In the darkness, he could clearly
hear the sobbing again, not below him now but all around.
Strangely, though, he felt that he could bear it if he had to,
horrible as it was.

Before turning in for the night, he knelt down and said
a short prayer for his family and fellow prisoners. Then he
lay down on the small, hard cot and swiftly entered into
dreams about better days, far off in the past.

one

Germany at War

The Bonhoeffer family sat around a large, black table in the dining room of their house in the Grunewald district of Berlin. Dr. Karl Bonhoeffer and his wife, Paula, sat at opposite ends of the table. Between them were arrayed six children, four of whom were their own and the other two were neighbors from down the street, Hans and Grete Dohnanyi.

The children were not allowed to talk during dinner unless they were spoken to first, but they often communicated to each other in their own special sign language across the table. Of course, they only did this when Dr. Bonhoeffer was not talking. Dietrich and Hans often held up different numbers of fingers to indicate what sort of game they wanted to play after dinner. One finger meant tag, two fingers meant toy soldiers, and so on.

This night, Dr. Bonhoeffer had a lot on his mind, and the children could sense his agitation. Contrary to his normal demeanor, he was complaining.

"The students all want to be *scientists*," he said, "but none of them is willing to do the work that is necessary to become a real scientist. They all like to analyze one another, but if I ask them to read a single book, it's as if I were sentencing them to the torture chamber!"

"Oh, Father," Paula gently chided. "It can't be all that bad. I'm sure you have very many fine students."

"Ah, but it is not like when I myself was a student at the university," Dr. Bonhoeffer answered. "We thought nothing of studying all day and even all night long. And by candlelight, mind you!"

Hans made a funny face, and Dietrich giggled, but his father seemed not to notice.

Paula did, though.

"Perhaps Dietrich will be a great scientist someday," she said, looking intently at her youngest son. "I'm sure the long hours of study would not bother him at all."

Dietrich grimaced.

"Yes, a younger generation will have to restore the glory of Germany, and of German scholarship," Dr. Bonhoeffer announced. "If Dietrich is a part of that, it would make me very proud indeed."

Dietrich simply nodded at his father. Even at his young age, he knew that he had no interest in scientific pursuits. He was not like his older brothers, Klaus and Karl-Friedrich, who enjoyed the rigors of the laboratory, or even Walter, who had enlisted in the German infantry. Walter had a tender sensitivity toward nature, an aspect of his personality that was undeniably being ravaged by the devastation he was seeing from the trenches.

But Dietrich was not as interested in the natural world

as he was in the world his mother revealed to him when she read aloud from a book of Bible stories. The supernatural world of the stories, inhabited by men and women of God, fascinated him. It seemed like an exciting world indeed. Prophets calling down fire from heaven. A shepherd boy slaying a monstrous giant. It made Dietrich think about what it would be like to be a man of God himself.

Whenever he tried to talk about the Bible stories with his older brothers, they laughed at him. "You'll grow out of your fascination with God someday," Karl-Friedrich would say. Or Klaus would say, "Don't you know that those are just fairy tales?"

But Dietrich's mother had read Hans Christian Andersen to him, also, and the Bible stories seemed like more than just fairy tales. Even though he could not articulate his feelings then, Dietrich sensed that the Bible stories spoke of a reality that was greater, wider, and more dramatic than the reality of scientists. One day, Klaus referred to Dietrich as "my brother, the theologian," and a seed was planted.

Over time, Dietrich learned to keep his speculations and musings about God to himself. They percolated inside him, though, and invaded his dreams.

After dinner the family retired to the parlor, where Dietrich, his sisters, and Hans acted out a play called "The Wild Swans." Dr. and Mrs. Bonhoeffer clapped excitedly at the end while the children took dramatic bows. Then Paula gathered them around her and began to teach them some old German folk songs. Dietrich and Hans sucked on candies while they listened impatiently to Paula's singing. They wanted to be off playing hide-and-seek.

Then there was a sudden knock at the front door. All of

the servants were busy, so Dr. Bonhoeffer put his newspaper aside to go answer it. Since it was rare to receive visitors unannounced at that time in the evening, Paula looked up at her husband a bit apprehensively as he walked into the hall. Even as she continued to sing to the children, she tried to overhear the conversation at the door. But her husband was speaking in hushed tones.

Finally, Dr. Bonhoeffer reentered the parlor, his face the color of ashes. As it was not his habit to shield the children from the harsh facts of life and death, Dr. Bonhoeffer began to read out loud a telegram from the German High Command. Paula felt a heavy sob rising in her chest as she guessed at the awful truth.

Walter had been killed at the front lines in France.

That night Dietrich and his twin sister, Sabine, lay awake in bed. They had always slept in the same bedroom, but on this night they were too sad and afraid even to be separated by the floor between their beds. The news about Walter seemed unreal. They could not believe it was true.

Their mother had left the parlor immediately after looking at the telegram. Dietrich would always remember the look on her face. Her eyes seemed to be looking everywhere and nowhere all at once. Their father had tried to comfort the children for a few minutes, but then he had joined his wife in her grief. The children's governess, Julie Horn, looked after them for the rest of the evening.

"I don't think I want to live in Germany my whole life," Sabine said in the dark.

"Why not?" Dietrich asked.

"Because Germany is always in a war. That's all we ever hear about at school, and all we ever hear about over the radio. War, war, war. I want to marry a rich businessman and travel around the world."

"But you are going to marry a *German* businessman, aren't you?" Dietrich asked.

"Maybe. Yes, I guess so," Sabine admitted.

"That's good," Dietrich said. "I would hate for you to move away." Then he thought a moment and said, "But no matter what you do, you will probably have a more exciting life than I will, especially if I do what Father wants me to do."

Sabine sighed. "Oh, Dietrich, Father was only grousing about his students like he does at the end of every semester. It did not have anything to do with you. He knows that you'll never be a scientist. You don't even like to pick up spiders."

"You're right," Dietrich answered, shuddering. "Spiders are hideous."

They lay in silence awhile more.

"Do you think I will ever get to be as old as Grandmother Tafel?" Sabine suddenly asked.

"No," Dietrich announced, "because Grandma Tafel will also get older as you do. You can never catch up."

"Dietrich! You know what I mean!"

Dietrich remained silent. He wasn't sure that he did know what she meant. Then his thoughts drifted back to Walter. He tried to imagine him in heaven, though he didn't know enough about heaven to see it clearly in his mind. Maybe it was like Berlin but with angels walking down the streets. Then he thought of his mother again, and of the horrible way her face had twisted in grief when she heard the news. Would she look like that if *he* died, Dietrich thought.

He remembered how he had plotted the progress of the

war on a large board, using red markers for the German army and black markers for the enemy. Like it was all a wonderful game. Now he would rather pick up a spider than use the markers again.

"I think you will do great things someday, Dietrich," Sabine said in a different tone of voice. "You are too good of a brother not to."

Dietrich was stymied by the praise from his twelve-year-old sister. All he could say was, "Thank you, Sabine. I think that you will do great things, too."

"Someday," his sister replied.

"Yes, someday," Dietrich agreed.

And as moonlight passed across the window shade at the end of the bed, brother and sister both fell gradually to sleep.

In the rooms below, their mother and father shook with grief, while hundreds of miles away the sounds of war continued to thunder.

two

School Days

T he classroom was dark because it was cloudy outside. Even on sunny days, the high, small windows
on one wall barely let in enough light. And the several candles scattered throughout the room seemed to be
tamped down by the heavy air. The students often had to
hold their books close to their faces to be able to read the
words.

Since the end of the war, all electrical power had been
rationed for use in Germany's struggling industrial plants.
The former manufacturers of guns, artillery, and fighter
planes were now supposed to rebuild Germany's scattered
economy by producing goods that could be sold throughout
Europe, and even to Germany's former enemies. Schools,
especially those to which the upper classes sent their children, did not bring an immediate benefit to the economy and
thus did not get any electricity.

In the classroom, twenty pupils sat in neat rows at small,

pine desks. Sabine sat two seats in front of Dietrich. Most of their classmates were children of university professors, just as they were. Even though they were all bright students, they tended to pay little attention to their beleaguered teacher, a half-Jewish Austrian named Klein-Schmidt. On this particular day, Klein-Schmidt had given up on the planned grammar lesson since most of the class was making paper airplanes instead of listening to him.

"All right," the teacher said, clearing his throat and gaining the class's attention. "Since you are not interested in grammar today, I am interested in finding out something about you."

While the rest of the class looked at their teacher skeptically, Dietrich stared out one of the windows, where a single ray of sun had broken through the gray mist.

"Most of you will be able to do anything you want to do with your lives," Klein-Schmidt continued. "You will be the ones, God help us, who will be responsible for restoring the glory of the German people."

The class groaned and giggled.

"I want to know what you plan to do with your lives—assuming you get passing grades this year." The class groaned again. "I really mean it now. What do you want to be when you grow up?" *And they have a lot of growing up to do,* he thought to himself.

A chubby boy in the front thrust his thick arm into the air.

"Yes, Helmut," the teacher said.

"I want to be a general so that I can sit around, smoke cigars, and order my soldiers to kill more Englishmen."

The class erupted into laughter.

"All right! All right!" The teacher walked down the rows, regaining some semblance of order.

22

"What about you, Elsa?" he said, pointing to a blond-haired girl in the row farthest from the windows.

"I want to be a doctor, like my father," Elsa replied.

"Girls can't be doctors," Helmut said, and the class broke into giggles once again.

"Lars, you're a smart lad. What do you want to do?" the teacher asked with a smile, pointing to a broad-shouldered boy in the back.

Lars thought for a moment and said, "I want to be a leader." Then he paused and said, "I don't care what type of leader it is; I just want to make things better for people like my aunt and uncle who live in Hartz. They have no money and are starving. I want to make Germany strong again, for them."

The boys in the class began to cheer, and even Klein-Schmidt could not help but get caught up in the emotion of Lars's statement. He puffed out his chest and nodded his head as he continued to walk up and down the rows. Finally he stopped next to Dietrich, who was still dreamily looking at the ray of light coming through the small window.

"And you, Bonhoeffer? What do *you* want to do with your life?"

Without hesitating, Dietrich responded, "I want to be a theologian."

Klein-Schmidt acted stunned, and even the class was silent for a moment. Then Helmut started to giggle, and the whole class caught the bug, all except Sabine whose face was red.

"Hmm, a theologian?" Klein-Schmidt said as he walked to the front of the classroom.

Now Dietrich's face was red, too. He wasn't sure why he had said what he said. He knew that most of his classmates' families did not go to church, or even pretend to believe in God. He tried to examine his feelings in the midst of the laughter. Perhaps he had said "theologian" because his mother had read to him from the Gospels—specifically, the Sermon on the Mount—the night before, and the fascinating words were still lingering in his head. Yet something deep within him told him that he had answered truthfully; that among all the possibilities, he wanted to study about God and the Church. He looked up at his teacher, who stood in front of the class with a smirk on his face.

"A theologian, eh?" Klein-Schmidt said, his voice heavy with sarcasm. "Well, you certainly shall have an *interesting* life."

As the class erupted into laughter again, Dietrich looked at the window. The ray of light was gone.

That evening at the dinner table, Sabine told the family about what had happened at school. Karl-Friedrich and Klaus snickered and jabbed each other with their elbows.

"I never knew you were interested in theology," Dietrich's father said to him.

"I wish I hadn't said it," Dietrich said meekly. "Everybody laughed."

"My grandfather was a great theologian," said Paula.

"Yes, but your grandfather lived during a different time in history," replied her husband, Karl. "People respected religion then, and even the intellectuals took it seriously. I'm afraid that most people would find it to be irrelevant today."

"Amen!" Karl-Friedrich said loudly, and he and Klaus laughed again.

"But if I am good at it, can't I *make* it relevant?" Dietrich shot back.

Karl smiled. "Well, all I am saying is that you will have a big task. And I would hate for you to be secluded away at a provincial church when you could be using your talents to shape the world."

"But Papa," Paula broke in, "surely the parishioners at a small church are still important and need to be cared for."

"I wasn't saying that they aren't important and don't deserve a good pastor," Karl replied. "I am just stating the fact that there must be thousands of young men who could fulfill that role. I'm not sure it would be the best place for someone like Dietrich, who has so many advantages."

There was a pause before Dietrich spoke. "I did not say that I wanted to be a pastor, Father. I want to be a theologian. I want to learn what great minds have said about God. It is a very intellectual profession, just like philosophy, science, and law."

Before the two older boys could argue that point, Karl said, "Perhaps. . .I suppose that if anyone can resuscitate a dead field, it may be someone as determined and as spontaneous as you, Dietrich."

Karl looked at his wife with bemusement, and Paula smiled. "Eat your soup, Dietrich," she said. "It's getting cold."

three

The Hedgehogs

Dietrich had been enrolled as a student at the University of Tübingen for only a couple of weeks when he was approached by an older student dressed all in black. Dietrich had seen such students around campus, and he had known that sooner or later they would get around to approaching him.

"Bonhoeffer, isn't it?" the student asked, extending his hand.

When Dietrich nodded, the other student continued. "My name is Rolf Hoftstag. I wanted to invite you to join the Hedgehog fraternity. I had heard that your father was a member."

"Yes, he was," Dietrich replied, somewhat reluctantly.

The Hedgehogs was one of the most prestigious fraternities at Tübingen. Openings in its ranks were normally reserved for sons of aristocratic Prussian families, and indeed, many prominent German leaders had been

Hedgehogs during their university days. It was an honor to be asked to join. Still, Dietrich was not sure if he wanted to devote himself to any fraternity. He only wanted to spend his time studying, perhaps taking time out to get together with family and friends for occasional social events.

But there was another side to being a member that troubled Dietrich. The Hedgehogs also included military training as part of their activities, and Dietrich was not sure that he would enjoy that.

"What do you say, Bonhoeffer?" Hoftstag asked. "I'm sure that your father would be proud."

"I have no doubt about that," Dietrich replied.

Then he did not say anything, creating an awkward silence. To refuse was almost unthinkable, and Dietrich was not so self-confident as to go against expectations. He also thought that he might possibly enjoy the camaraderie that the Hedgehogs would provide. The fraternity, which sought to combine scholarship and manliness, certainly appealed to his idea of what it meant to be a German.

"Sure," he finally said to Hoftstag. "I would love to join the Hedgehogs."

"Great!" Hoftstag said, beaming. "Then we will see you at Puschdorf Hall tonight for initiation. Don't worry, it's not too bad." Then he slapped Dietrich on the shoulder and strode away, leaving the newest Hedgehog feeling queasy in the pit of his stomach.

Soon, Dietrich found himself spending a couple of evenings during the week practicing his shooting and sword fighting. Once a month, the Hedgehogs held mock battles on the fields that surrounded the campus, and Dietrich, to his surprise, found himself enjoying the strenuous, physical part of these exercises. He was stronger than many of the fraternity brothers and could hold his own on the field. He also entertained notions that he wouldn't be half-bad as a real soldier if given the chance.

Though many of the Hedgehog activities did seem childish and boorish to him, especially the weekend beer parties, he was only seventeen, barely beyond childhood himself. Who was he to judge them? He took to wearing the customary all-black clothes of the Hedgehogs around campus and began to slack off in his reading. *So what if my studies are suffering a bit*, he thought to himself. *University life is more than just books and lectures*. Yet by midterm, it was clear that his grades were already well below what he had hoped for.

One night during midterm week, Dietrich sat in the library in his black Hedgehog jacket, worrying over a philosophy text. The chapter he was reading concerned the problem of whether the *existence* of something could be separated from its *essence*. It was an old philosophical problem, yet Dietrich was finding it almost impossible to grasp the idea.

Suddenly a young man sat down next to him. Dietrich was startled, and even a bit annoyed, by the abrupt intrusion into his privacy. Glancing over at the young man, who had dark features and deep-set eyes, Dietrich gave a terse greeting.

"Hello," the young man answered. "I just wanted to comment on the nice jacket you are wearing."

Dietrich leaned back in his chair. It was obvious, with his concentration broken, that he wasn't going to be given the chance to understand the difference between existence and essence that evening.

"Why, thank you," Dietrich said, barely stifling a yawn. "It's a Hedgehog jacket."

"I know," the young man replied.

"Oh, are you a member?" Dietrich asked, embarrassed to realize that the young man might be a fraternity brother whom he hadn't met yet.

But the young man replied with a slight smile. "Oh, no, I'm not a Hedgehog." Then he paused before stating emphatically, "My name is Sol Friesberg."

Dietrich was confused. Was he supposed to know the young Mr. Friesberg? "I'm sorry. I'm a first-year student and don't know many people around campus yet," Dietrich said.

"Just Hedgehogs?" Sol asked, not looking at Dietrich.

"Yes, I primarily know Hedgehogs," Dietrich replied, still thoroughly confused. "Why? Were you interested in joining? If so, I might be able to help."

But his question brought a loud bark of laughter from Sol. "I'm sorry, uh. . ."

"Bonhoeffer," Dietrich said.

"I'm sorry, Bonhoeffer," Sol continued, "but I shall never have the privilege of becoming a Hedgehog. You see, I'm the head of the Jewish student group on campus."

"I'm afraid I don't understand," Dietrich said, now becoming annoyed.

"I'm sorry, but I believe that the Hedgehogs would rather have a dog join their fraternity than a Jew," Sol said, giving him a deadly serious look.

"You must be mistaken. I've never heard any slander against Jews at our meetings."

"Ah, yes," said Sol. "And how long have you been attending the meetings? No matter, you can check with the leadership. I'm sure they will set you straight about their 'Jewish policy.' " He said the last two words derisively.

"Yes, I will check, Herr Friesberg," Dietrich responded

in a weak voice.

"Call me Sol," the young man said as he rose to leave. "And by the way, Bonhoeffer, I do admire your jacket. You must be very proud."

Dietrich sat alone again in the middle of the library. Sol's words reverberated in his head. *Could it be true that the Hedgehogs are truly haters of Jews*, he asked himself. Then he remembered the songs he sang in Hedgehog meetings about "Germany, pure and strong," "The blood of Christian men," and so forth, whose underlying meanings and connotations he now saw in a different light. He had thought the songs were merely patriotic, not hateful.

Suddenly it seemed like his entire world had come crashing down. He closed his philosophy book, laid his head down upon it, and began to weep softly.

Dietrich left Tübingen at the end of his first year and enrolled at the University of Berlin. Even though he was breaking with family tradition, he enjoyed the intellectual atmosphere of Berlin much more than the anti-Semitic atmosphere of Tübingen. In Berlin, he was not expected to join a fraternity. He was only expected to study as hard as he could, which was an activity he did not mind at all.

During that first year back in Berlin, Dietrich's mind swam with new ideas. His professors were the best in the world, or at least they said they were, and he hung on their every word as if they were prophets of God. As his confidence grew, he began to speak up in class.

One day in a class on German literature, Dietrich raised his hand in the middle of the lecture. The professor had been talking about Goethe's play *Faust*, and Dietrich had been struck by the way Goethe opposed nature to civilization. It seemed like the great poet was calling upon men to throw off civilization and return to the primitivism of the wild. And yet, Dietrich wasn't sure since Goethe's phrases could sometimes be understood in opposite ways. The professor, an ancient man who had first read Goethe thirty years before Dietrich's birth, noticed him and called his name.

"I was just wondering," Dietrich began, "if Goethe knew that his ideas were dangerous to the state, I mean, to the government at that time?"

The professor suppressed a smile. "I think Goethe was very well aware of the political implications of his ideas. But he knew that most of the political leaders wouldn't be able to understand them anyway. So he just went about his business."

A few students in the class snickered, knowing that the old professor was simply playing with the exuberant, yellow-haired young man.

"But did he ever think that his poems would eventually cause a change in society?" Dietrich went on, unabashed.

"I don't know," the professor answered, "but I'm sure he was like the rest of us. All he could do was hope."

"Oh, I don't think he was like the rest of us at all," Dietrich responded. "I think he was a cut above the average man."

"Somewhat like yourself?" the professor said, with a twinkle in his eye.

Snickering broke out all over the room as Dietrich realized that he was debating about Goethe with someone who had been teaching the subject twice as long as he had been alive. He sank back in his chair.

"Come to my office later, young Bonhoeffer," the professor said. "I will discuss the aspirations of Goethe with you for as long as you like. But for now, I have to get this lecture done before dinner. If I don't, both of us will lose our audience."

Dietrich eventually did go to see the professor about Goethe. He also visited most of his other professors that year. He was a remarkable student who showed promise as a scholar from the first day. The professors were first amused and then accepting as Dietrich began to speak with them like an equal. He didn't know as much, but his ability to think, reason, and work his way toward original ideas in many cases surpassed theirs. When he was barely past his twentieth birthday, he was already being spoken of as a bright star on the horizon of German theology. It was assumed that he would immediately begin graduate studies upon the completion of his undergraduate courses, and he did. He excelled, too, which made his parents very proud and his siblings somewhat surprised.

The one thing missing from Dietrich's life during these years of intense theological and philosophical study, though, was a warm heart of true faith. He was learning everything that had ever been said about God, and yet he never spoke to God himself. He never prayed or read the Bible in order to hear what God was saying to him personally. Growing up in a highly intellectual atmosphere, he had absorbed the assumption that expressions of religious fervor were something the ignorant masses did. It was the province of those who lived according to their hearts, not according to their minds.

Toward the end of his graduate studies, though, two separate experiences conspired to challenge Dietrich's purely intellectual approach to Christianity.

The first happened in the summer of 1924, when

Dietrich and his brother Klaus traveled to Rome. They went as cultured Germans, eager to study the ancient ruins and catacombs. But Dietrich found himself increasingly distracted by the extreme Catholicism of the city's population. Everywhere he went he noticed expressions of devotion: shopkeepers and their wives lined up at outdoor confessionals, old women sitting on their doorsteps fingering prayer beads, the steady stream of pedestrians heading to early morning and late evening masses. He was struck by how Catholicism was not just a *part* of the people's lives but was the focal point of their existence.

In such an environment, the word "religion" lost all meaning. Being Catholic wasn't merely something that the people did, it was *who they were*. They were Catholics first and Italians second. Such devotion provided Dietrich with a compelling judgment against the social Protestantism of his own culture in which a person's religion was many times merely a part of his professional resumè. He began to reflect on the possibility that Germans were so proud of their religiosity that it was hard for them to be Christians.

After this trip, Dietrich would always admire Catholicism for its emphasis on the sacraments—those activities that brought the individual and the community into actual contact with the divine. And he would become especially fascinated by monastic practices, which he came to see as the best way of gaining a thoroughly *experiential* knowledge of God. In short, his trip to Rome showed him that Christianity was not entirely an affair of the mind but was also not merely an expression of culture. It was, more importantly, something to be believed in and lived among other believers. Christianity was the daily experience of God, both individually and corporately, to the furtherance of God's glory alone.

During these years, Dietrich also made contact with the most controversial theologian in the German world, a man named Karl Barth. Barth was controversial because he challenged the reigning liberalism of German theology. Almost everybody at the University of Berlin was a theological liberal, which meant that they focused on Christianity's historical development and were skeptical of biblical inerrancy. They also emphasized the social implications of Christianity. Barth, who had recently become famous through the publication of his commentary on the Epistle to the Romans, countered liberalism by emphasizing the changelessness of God and His Word. Through his many conversations with Barth, Dietrich gradually began to believe that Christians could have an independent and prophetic impact upon society if only God's Word were acknowledged for what it was—the communication of God's unchanging will to His lost creation.

Dietrich never entirely rejected the social gospel of liberalism, but after meeting Barth he thought that liberalism and Barthianism both had something important to say to modern Protestants. One taught the importance of having a concern for the social problems of contemporary society. The other taught that God's Word contained eternal answers. Dietrich thought that each point of view could not be divorced from the other, although it was difficult to bring them together in a properly theological way. His doctoral thesis was an attempt to perform this synthesis, but unfortunately, it would be many years before other scholars paid much attention to it. By the time a few theologians noticed, Dietrich was much more interested in living out the meaning of the Church than he was interested in talking about it.

four

"Religious Community"

Dietrich defended his doctoral thesis in December of 1927. The thesis, entitled *Sanctorum Communio,* was a technical work on the topic of "religious community," and it brought together liberalism and Barthianism while also growing out of his experiences among the Catholic community in Rome. During the last three years, he had read more books in a shorter period of time than he ever would again. He had become proficient not only in theology, but in philosophy and ethics, too. His childhood conviction that theology could be as intellectual and rigorous as scientific studies had been borne out.

Now with his academic work behind him, Dietrich was faced with the requirement of one year's practical ministry experience before his theology degree would be granted. The presbytery recommended that he fill an opening for an assistant pastor at a German-speaking church in Barcelona, Spain. It was a small congregation, but the regular pastor was enfeebled by age and needed a younger man to take up some of his visitation and preaching duties.

Dietrich was eager to see how he would fare in a non-academic environment, among parishioners who cared more about how well he could meet their spiritual needs than the prestige of his degree. Yet he was apprehensive about entering a world he knew nothing about. He was confident in his abilities, but he worried that the struggling bourgeoisie and poor laborers of Barcelona would not accept his ministry, or even listen to what he had to say.

One night over dinner, he discussed his apprehensions with his parents.

"It is simply a part of the requirements, Dietrich," Karl Bonhoeffer said as he cut into his veal. "It's something you just have to endure before you can continue with your academic career."

"Yes, I suppose," Dietrich replied while pushing his peas around on his plate.

"And I wouldn't worry about the receptiveness of the congregation," Dr. Bonhoeffer continued. "They will respect you because of how you carry yourself, and even if they don't say so, they will respect you for your intelligence and learning."

Dietrich nodded unenthusiastically.

"Besides," his mother added, "it will be a good opportunity to learn the culture. You can come back and explain to us the Spaniard's absurd fascination with the spectacle of bullfighting. It seems so barbaric and cruel. I hear that the Spaniards even bring their small children to the bullring."

Dietrich chuckled and said, "I don't know if I will ever be able to explain that aspect of Spanish culture." He paused for a moment. "But I am actually more interested in a different sort of mystery."

"Hmm. . .what's that?" his father asked as he vigorously chewed his broccoli.

Dietrich hesitated. He was wary of revealing to his parents some of the ideas and questions that his theological studies were awakening in his mind. They still thought of theology as a safe and somewhat secluded profession. In their minds, its basic irrelevance to the modern world was a positive feature. It meant that their youngest son would be protected from the increasingly dangerous and impersonal dynamics of a turbulent world. He would simply teach and write books that few people would ever read. He would also be part of a small, yet very supportive, community that was carrying on the German legacy in the abstract sciences.

"I guess I am interested," Dietrich tentatively began, "in whether the Church, *as the Church*, and individual Christians, *as Christians*, can make a real difference—a *redemptive* difference—in the communities they belong to, even among those outside the Church."

His parents stopped eating and merely looked at him.

"All right, Dietrich," his father smiled. "This is your chance to practice simplicity of speech. I fear that your mother and I are not quite grasping your point."

Paula cleared her throat. "If you are saying that Christianity and the Church are necessary for maintaining civilized values and a stable society," she said quietly, "I'm sure that we are in absolute agreement." Then she paused. "But I'm not sure that that is what you are meaning to say."

Dietrich took a drink of milk while contemplating his reply to his mother. His thoughts ran back to a time when, as a boy, he had brazenly declared to his science-minded brothers, "If the Church is irrelevant, then I will make it relevant!" He was a bit more realistic about the scope of that challenge now, but his attitude was fundamentally the same. He knew that he would always be restless in a cloistered profession. He had to be involved in changing things. Then again, the peacefulness of the library carrel also held great appeal for his inquisitive and scholarly mind. Understanding philosophical ideas and coming up with exciting new syntheses of information gave him a sense of joy unlike any other.

Frankly, he was divided.

"I do believe that the Church is one of the foundations of our civilization," he began. "Without the Church performing its sacramental and pastoral function, the forces of barbarism would be given free sway."

He paused before he went on.

"But I also think that the Church cannot remain a positive force if it continues to remove itself from the stress and strain of contemporary events. The Church has a prophetic role to play in the world, not just a pastoral role. The true Church and the world cannot always be on friendly terms, I believe. The sort of friendliness between Church and society that we have cultivated in the past, especially in Germany, is actually the cause of the Church's increasing irrelevance." He leaned forward on his elbows and clasped his hands. "What I mean to say is that on the important issues of life, the Church must stand up and be counted, even if it stands alone."

"Dietrich, I'm afraid I still don't understand where your vehemence is coming from," his father said with a sigh. "How do you propose that the Church involve itself in the *stress and strain of contemporary events?*"

Dietrich sat back in his chair. "I'm not sure," he finally said. "But it seems to me that since the Church is the only place where the Word of God is preached, it has a responsibility to preach the whole Word of God. And from my studies of the Bible, I know that God is rarely satisfied to confine Himself to merely *personal* issues between issues. He is interested in the whole world, and everything that goes on in it. He is not to be closeted somewhere, only to be brought out when we have questions science hasn't answered yet. That is a sure-fire recipe for irrelevance."

"But a pastor can't get involved in everything," Paula said.

"That may be true," Dietrich replied. "But I fear that our German pastors have been too afraid to get their hands dirty. By not getting involved in the real issues of the day, or even the real issues of people's daily lives, they have demonstrated, by example, that God can be shoved off to the margins of life. That may be a comfortable way of doing things, but it is not the full measure of the Church's calling. The Church is on the earth to embody the Word of God. As such, it must struggle to discover God's Word for each particular situation. I see this as the highest responsibility in the world."

"Are you saying that pastors should also be politicians, businessmen, and soldiers?" Karl asked.

"No," Dietrich replied. "But pastors should be able to proclaim Christ's Word to politicians, businessmen, and soldiers in a relevant way. A pastor should be able to show them how to put God in the center of their lives and thus make a difference for the kingdom."

"And how will you do that?" Paula asked.

At that Dietrich smiled. "I really have no idea. I just want to give it a try."

Karl and Paula Bonhoeffer remained silent as they looked at each other. Within each of their hearts, they realized that their headstrong youngest son would never be satisfied to sit on the sidelines, no matter what profession he chose. He would always be jumping right into the middle of the fray, just as he did when he had played ball as a child. Yet their concern was mingled with a burgeoning pride.

"I both envy and pity the church that will take you on as its pastor," Karl Bonhoeffer said, allowing a smile to creep around the edges of his mouth. "The congregation may be getting more than they had bargained for."

"Oh, Papa, you know that I am essentially harmless," Dietrich said while munching strongly on a chunk of dark bread.

At that, they all laughed together.

five

Barcelona

To Dietrich, the matador had a magical glow about him that was almost like an aura. His movements seemed like choreographed steps in a dance in which the bull was an unwilling partner. One could almost get lost in the colors: the darting and bobbing red of the cape, the brilliant bluish black of the bull's torso, and the skittering white of the matador's high stockings. The spectacle was beautiful, strange, thrilling, and yet somehow sickening, all at once.

Dietrich didn't know how he was going to explain the attraction and allure of bullfighting to his mother. There was something about being there so close to the life-and-death action that stirred Dietrich's soul. He wondered apprehensively if he were turning into a bit of an old-fashioned pagan.

The senior pastor of the German congregation, an elderly and stooped man by the name of Fritz Olbricht, had invited Dietrich to the bullfight, telling him that it would be a good way to learn about the Spanish soul. But Dietrich ended up learning a great deal more about his own soul. He found himself exulting in the bloody action along with the Reverend Olbricht, who stood at Dietrich's side and pumped his fists in the air with every thrust of the lance. Dietrich hoped that he himself admired only the aesthetic and visual purity of the event and not the controlled viciousness. But he wasn't so sure.

At least there was nothing pagan about his Sunday sermons. He worked on his messages diligently throughout the week, crafting and honing them to produce the desired effect. The problem was that it was always difficult to tell exactly how his messages were being received by the small congregation. Most of the merchants and farmers only wanted to talk about their businesses and farms, or about the political situation in Germany, where the Weimar Republic was crumbling into anarchy. This meant that all of his intricately reasoned discourses on Christ and the Church were probably falling on deaf, or at least unwilling, ears. And all of his prayers for a spiritual awakening among his exiled German parishioners seemed to be going unanswered. He didn't know how to break through to their hearts.

Yet he did not know how to preach any other way. Olbricht, who was generally supportive of Dietrich's efforts, told him that the Spanish culture had created in the Germans a thirst for the dramatic, and for sermons that had a practical connection to their daily affairs. "This is what Jesus Himself did, isn't it?" the senior pastor reminded him. "Don't try to be too intellectual."

But Dietrich did not think that he was being too intellectual. He felt compelled to confront the parishioners with the relevance of Jesus to the whole of their lives. He did not want to merely entertain them with stories, or give them practical advice on how to be better businessmen and farmers. He wanted to challenge them, and he believed that in their hearts they wanted to be challenged. Out of a colony of six thousand Germans in Barcelona, only about forty saw fit to attend services each Sunday. So the older minister could not have been doing everything right.

Dietrich knew, though, that he could only get more people to attend if he actually got involved in their lives and showed that he cared about them. So for the first few months, he tried to visit most of the three hundred people who were on the membership list of the church. He listened to complaints about neighbors and about the price of doing business in Spain. He sat in kitchens and drank cider with old widows. He went out to the playgrounds to frolic with the children.

Gradually the Sunday attendance increased. And once the people got a chance to hear Dietrich speak, they usually returned, even though he sometimes said things that rebuked the complacency in their lives. He cut to the heart of the difference between religion and faith, characterizing "religion" as a mere accessory to life, and true faith as that which stood at the center of a person's soul and affected their whole way of life, their basic attitudes.

For example, one Sunday he preached about the nearness of Christ:

> *Jesus is with us in His Word. . .in what He*
> *wishes and thinks about us. . . . Jesus Christ,*
> *God Himself, addresses us through every man;*
> *the other human being, that puzzling, inscrutable*

> *thou, is God's call to us, God Himself Who comes to meet us. . . .*
>
> *. . .Christ will wander upon earth as long as men exist, as your neighbor, as He through whom God calls you, speaks to you, makes demands on you. That is the great urgency and the great joy of the Advent message, that Christ is at the door, lives among us in human form. Will you close or open the door to Him?*

Another Sunday, as Dietrich stood at the back of the church and shook hands with the exiting parishioners, a woman who always vaguely reminded him of his mother took his arm and pulled him close. In a mixture of Spanish and German she said, "I wonder, Pastor Bonhoeffer, if you would be willing to pay my son a visit?" Her voice carried an undertone of pain.

"I would be happy to, Frau Richter," Dietrich responded. "Does your son live with you?"

"Well, he keeps his bed in my house," she said, "but most of the time he is in the saloon [a word she spat out like an oath]. You would have to catch him in the early afternoon—after he wakes up, but before he leaves again."

"Your son likes to drink, eh?"

"It's not a matter anymore of liking it or not liking it," Frau Richter said morosely. "It's simply what he does."

Dietrich looked deeply into the eyes of the widow, a woman who had lost her beloved husband in the Great War and who looked much older than her fifty years. He thought of Jesus' own interactions with grieving widows and parents. They came to Him asking for the impossible, and He never turned a single one away. Dietrich also thought of how the ministry of Jesus had been passed on to the Church. It was an awesome responsibility, and not one that could be rationalized away.

"I will be there tomorrow afternoon after lunch," he said.

Frau Richter's mouth creased into a tight smile as she said, "Gracias, Señor Bonhoeffer," and released his arm. Then, pausing on the steps of the church, she added, "I will make sure that Josef is ready for you."

Dietrich watched her hurry out onto the sidewalk. He tried to follow her bobbing head down the street but soon lost her among the bustling crowd. Sunday was a popular shopping day in Barcelona, and the streets were filled.

Then Dietrich turned his attention back to the parishioners and continued to shake hands until everyone was gone.

The Richter residence was on the outskirts of both Barcelona and of the German community there. From the church, it was about a twelve-block walk. Dietrich arrived at a quarter past one, and Frau Richter served him coffee and strudel before disappearing into a room near the rear of the small apartment. Dietrich took the opportunity to survey the sparse furnishings, which consisted mainly of flea-market items that bespoke a poverty he was not accustomed to. But his observations were soon interrupted by a young man's garbled voice emanating from the back room. Dietrich understood a sufficient number of Spanish curse words to know that the man was not happy with his mother at that moment.

Then there was silence.

Frau Richter soon emerged from the dark room with some hair disentangled from her normally tight bun. "I'm sorry," she said. "Josef is incorrigible today. You would never know that he is a twenty-three-year-old man. He acts like a spoiled child of six."

Dietrich tried to hide his inner uneasiness. He was still inexperienced in dealing with domestic problems, and it was disconcerting that he was being asked to counsel a man who was different from him in every way, except age. The situation was intimidating.

"Should I go back and talk with him?" Dietrich asked.

Frau Richter looked at him with eyes close to tears and quietly said, "yes."

Dietrich rose from his chair and walked quickly across the room. He wanted to appear confident, but he was anything but. So before entering the darkened room, he said a short prayer under his breath.

Before he could enter, though, Josef pushed past him and shuffled into the kitchen area.

"Is there any coffee, Mama?" the young man asked in a throaty voice. He had curly brown hair and looked Spanish despite his German parentage.

"Here, let me get it for you," Dietrich said, going to a coffeepot that sat on top of a coal stove. "You look tired. Why don't you sit down?"

Josef, still groggy, obeyed.

Dietrich found a cup and brought the coffee to the table, where he poured for everyone.

"Josef, your mother asked me to come here to talk to you."

Josef grunted as he slurped the coffee.

"I have something to ask of you," Dietrich continued unabated. "I would like you to come to church this Sunday with your mother."

46

Josef stopped drinking and smirked. "But I am very busy on Sunday mornings."

"Yes, I am sure you are," Dietrich said, sitting down. "But as I was walking here today, I noticed something. It occurred to me that there are some neighborhoods between here and the church that a woman should not walk through alone. I would think that, as the man of the house, you would feel a responsibility to make sure that your mother gets to church safely. Am I right in assuming that?"

Josef did not respond, and Dietrich leaned toward him. "Your mother will certainly not stop coming to church—not a good Christian woman like her."

Josef's eyes narrowed like slits. He had never been confronted by anyone like the sturdy young pastor with the thick German accent. Since Dietrich was challenging his manhood, Josef's first instinct was to attack, to drive the minister back to where he came from. But then he considered Dietrich's strong looking shoulders and hands, and the steel blue determination in his eyes.

"And since it is such a long hike, there will be no time to walk home and back again before the service is over, especially since my sermons are especially short," Dietrich said, looking at Frau Richter, who was beaming.

"All I am saying," he went on, suddenly serious, "is that I myself would not want to see my own mother exposed to danger and left unprotected. I would not be able to forgive myself if some tragedy befell her."

Josef rose and declared that he was going back to bed.

"Yes, perhaps you should sleep on it," Dietrich replied, as the surly young man trudged off to the back room again.

Dietrich wasn't sure how his challenge had been received, but the next Sunday morning the young man sat next to his mother in her regular pew. Moreover, he was awake as he sat there.

From the pulpit, it even looked as if he was listening.

Without ever having fully understood the allure of bull-fighting, Dietrich left Spain in November of 1928. After his ten months there, he felt like a more well-rounded individual. His experiences had opened him up to the problems and challenges of ordinary people. He had learned how to communicate God's Word in a simple yet effective way, and how to survive on his own. At the age of twenty-two, he was finally feeling like a responsible adult rather than a precocious student. Yet his new experiences were not to end with his time in Barcelona.

The next year he was off to America.

six

Visit to America

C an you tell us about the situation of the Jews in
your country, Mr. Bonhoeffer?"

The question had been posed by the eminent
theologian Reinhold Niebuhr, who was one of Dietrich's
primary sponsors during his stay at Union Theological
Seminary in New York City. Dietrich was there on a one-
year Sloan Fellowship to attend some graduate classes and
to learn about American theology.

What he saw and heard did not impress him right away.
The professors at Union seemed to be unaware of what the
great contemporary European theologians like Karl Barth
were saying. Sometimes it seemed to Dietrich as if they
were willfully ignorant, stressing the importance of experience, politics, and economics almost to the total exclusion of
any dogmatic statements about God, Christ, the Church, or
Scripture.

Yet their emphasis on a practical Christianity did lead

the professors (especially Niebuhr) to be interested in ethics, one of Dietrich's pet subjects. Instead of talking about ethics in abstract language, Niebuhr and his colleagues thought that ethical statements were worthless unless they told how to change one's immediate environment for the better, or the right thing to do in a real-world situation.

Thus the question surfaced about the Jews.

As fifteen graduate students in theology and their esteemed professor sat waiting, Dietrich tried to organize his thoughts. For some reason, he had the sneaking suspicion that Niebuhr was asking him this question for a specific and double-edged purpose. Perhaps the professor knew more than Dietrich about the Jewish situation and was merely testing him. Dietrich had already learned that old Reinhold was a cagey character who would not be satisfied with an incomplete answer to his question.

So Dietrich decided to begin on a personal note.

"Four years ago, my twin sister, Sabine, married a Jew, though one who was baptized as a Christian. His name is Gerhard Leibholz, and he is a very talented constitutional lawyer."

Dietrich paused to notice how intently the class was listening to him.

"The shame is that Gerhard will not be able to rise in his profession as far as is warranted by his talent," he continued. "There is, I am sorry to say, a great deal of irrational prejudice against Jews in my country. The ordinary Germans are still suffering the aftereffects of our defeat in the Great War. Or rather, they are still suffering from the effects of the so-called peace treaty that ended the war."

Speaking to an American audience as he was, Dietrich expected his last comment to elicit some grumbling among the students, but there was nary a whisper of dissent. Most of them were probably intelligent enough, he thought, to be objective about the actual nature of the "peace" treaty that had reduced Germany to unprecedented levels of poverty.

"Of course, the unfairness and bitter terms of the treaty are no excuse for blaming most of our national problems on one ethnic group. But Germans have a great deal of pride and cannot bear humiliation very well. It was easy to predict that our degradation would seek out a scapegoat."

Niebuhr cleared his throat to interrupt, and Dietrich nodded in his direction.

"I have heard that the far right is experiencing a resurgence in Germany, especially in Munich and the Bohemian region. Can you confirm that?" Niebuhr asked.

Dietrich smiled at how well informed his host was. "There are groups who call themselves nationalists and who like to do a lot of shouting and brawling in the beer halls. Some of them are becoming politically organized and are pushing for seats in the Reichstag. The insidious part of it," Dietrich said, recalling his own days at Tübingen, "is that they are very influential among the young people. Many of the younger German nationalists have rallied around a man who failed to overthrow the government seven years ago. You may have heard of him—his name is Adolf Hitler."

"Of course," Niebuhr gravely replied.

"Are the German churches speaking out against the prejudice and abuse that the Jews are experiencing?"

The questioner was a fastidiously dressed young black man who sat uncomfortably in his chair.

"Well, Mr. . .uh. . ."

"Fisher," the student replied. "Frank Fisher."

"I wish I could say that the churches are making an

51

ethical stand on the issue, Mr. Fisher," Dietrich warmly replied, "but the truth is that most German Christians are not too worried about the suffering, both actual and potential, of minority groups."

"Sounds a lot like America," Fisher said, smiling, while a number of students chuckled.

Dietrich was momentarily confused. He had always been told that America was the land of democracy and equal rights for all. Whatever it lacked in terms of refined culture and profound scholarship, America always had the advantage, at least in Dietrich's mind, of being a great melting pot where the least-advantaged immigrant or minority member could gradually, through hard work and persistence, rise to a prominent place in society. He said to his questioner, "Surely the prejudice against minorities in America is superficial and can be overcome through the democratic process."

At this Frank Fisher almost bounced out of his seat with mirth, and even Professor Niebuhr couldn't suppress a wry smile.

The theologian, rather than the student, answered Dietrich first. "It is a little more complicated than that," Niebuhr said evenly, "although I have faith that the democratic process, as you say, will someday prevail."

Frank Fisher finally settled down in his chair. "I've got to take you to Harlem, Man; it'll blow you out of the water."

"Har. . .Ha. . .I'm sorry, that is a difficult word for a German to pronounce. Where is this place?"

"Just a couple blocks from here," Fisher said, pointing with his thumb out the window. "We can take a little stroll over there tomorrow."

"On a Sunday?" Dietrich asked. "Are you sure?"

"Best day to go, Man," Fisher said, nodding his head. "Best day to go."

The next morning at nine o'clock it was already eighty degrees out on the sidewalks of New York. Dietrich and Frank walked together from the campus of Union Seminary to the Abyssinian Baptist Church in Harlem. Along the way, Frank began to explain the facts of segregation in America and Dietrich ravenously soaked up the information. The parallels to the Jewish situation in Germany were striking—the segregation, discrimination, and political persecution. Dietrich resolved then and there to learn all he could about black America.

By the time they got to the church, the worship service was well underway. Dietrich was at first amazed and then delighted by the clapping, shouting, and dancing of the congregation as they sang songs of praise, the words of which Dietrich had never seen in the Lutheran hymnal. In Rome, he had witnessed the fervency of Italian Catholics, men and women who wept as they prayed, but this was something altogether new.

Frank leaned close to Dietrich. "The folks here love to worship God."

Dietrich nodded, and Frank continued, "Sometimes they go on for an hour or more, just singing and carrying on. They say that if you can't *feel* the Lord, you haven't found Him yet."

Before long, Dietrich could not resist anymore and entered into the spirit of the service himself, clapping and shouting along with everybody else. Then, as the singing segued seamlessly into a call-and-response message by the robed minister, he found himself "amening" at the top of his lungs. By the end of the two-hour service, Dietrich walked out of the church exhausted and drenched with perspiration.

"I've never been in anything like that before," he said to Frank as they made their way to a nearby steakhouse for lunch.

"Well, nobody would have known it," Frank said, laughing. "You looked like you had grown up in the black church. I even had to check halfway through to make sure your skin was still white."

Dietrich laughed, too. "I'm sure I stood out in the crowd, though."

"Yeah," Frank said as he opened the door of the steakhouse for his new German friend. "Like a fox in a chicken coop."

Dietrich was not the only European student and theologian at Union that year on a Sloan Fellowship. Jean Lassere, a quiet Frenchman, attended the same classes as Dietrich and, through his scattered comments, gave Dietrich the impression that he was also knowledgeable about the intellectual currents then sweeping over the Old World. In that sense, he was more sophisticated than the average American graduate student.

At first, Dietrich and Lassere avoided each other outside of class. Since there was still a great deal of tension between Germany and France, neither knew how to approach the other. As the sole representatives of their respective countries, they carried a burden not only of strangeness but also of history.

It was especially difficult considering that one of Dietrich's goals in New York had been to educate Americans about the unfairness and terrible consequences of the treaty that had ended the Great War. Forced upon the Germans largely by the French, the treaty had been a crushing blow to Germany's dignity and resources. The situation created by it had allowed a political vacuum to develop that was being filled by right-wing, militarist groups. And Dietrich was not willing to water down his opinions about this just because there was a Frenchman in his classes.

The two young men were also polar opposites in appearance and temperament. Lassere was slight and dark, while Dietrich was large boned, muscular, and blond. The Frenchman tended to be elegant and refined in his manners, while Dietrich could easily present an aggressive front, though he had no intention of coming across like that. He was simply boisterous at times, like an overgrown puppy. These differences made it inevitable that the two men would have a confrontation.

It happened one afternoon in a class on Christian ethics. The class, which was Dietrich's favorite, provided a forum for combative discussion on a subject in which the Americans actually excelled. And as Dietrich's ability to converse in English grew, so did his ability to hold his own in an argument. He took joy in contrasting a Lutheran perspective to the grab-bag theology of his American peers.

This particular afternoon, the topic was Augustine's concept of the just war.

The professor, an amiable man who was growing used to Dietrich's enthusiastic confidence, had been unable to talk for a full five minutes at the beginning of class before he was interrupted.

"I think that Luther provided a nice extension of Augustine's categories into the premodern world," Dietrich broke in when the professor paused to take a breath. "He showed how important it was for theology to be able to speak to that most worldly of acts: the act of war."

"Yes, well. . . ," said the professor before Dietrich continued his monologue.

"Luther was especially adept at showing how the pervasiveness of original sin makes war an inevitability, or even a necessity for—"

"It is not a necessity that the free man take part in it," Lassere spoke out from the back of the room.

Dietrich swiveled his head around, and his eyes met the Frenchman's unblinking stare. "What do you mean by *the free man?*" Dietrich asked tentatively.

"I mean the man who is free to obey Scripture over the dictates of any purely national conflict," Lassere answered evenly, in clearly enunciated English.

The rest of the class seemed to fade away for Dietrich as he turned to face his fellow European more squarely. He was sure that Lassere was not just expressing an alternative position but rather, absolute heresy. How could a Christian refuse to go to war if his country called upon him? Wasn't it a sacred duty?

"But don't you believe that the Christian holds dual citizenship, both in the kingdom of God *and* in this world?" he asked fiercely.

"Yes, I do," Lassere replied. "But since the kingdom of God extends throughout this whole world in the hearts of Christian believers, I refuse to make such an easy distinction between the two realms."

Dietrich decided to get to the heart of the matter. "So if France were unjustly invaded by an enemy power and called upon you to defend her, and your family, against the threat of annihilation, you would refuse?" He paused for effect before continuing. "And would not your refusal mean that someone else was potentially putting his life on the line in your place?"

Lassere did not answer right away. It was obvious that the question pained him. "I'm not saying that it would be easy," he finally said. "I love my country as much as you love yours." Another short pause followed. "But I would have to refuse nonetheless—"

"On what grounds?" Dietrich shot back.

"On the grounds that my participation in the war would force me to participate in killing my brothers in the Lord."

Now it was Dietrich's turn to be silent. He was stunned by this way of viewing things.

"Nothing in Scripture gives a Christian the right to destroy the body of Christ, no matter what authority he may appeal to," Lassere continued. "Do we believe in the holy, universal Church, the community of saints? Or do we believe in the eternal mission of France, or of Germany? I must confess, Herr Bonhoeffer, that in my mind it is impossible to be both a Christian and a nationalist."

Dietrich sat staring at Lassere, his confusion evident on his face. "I will have to read and think on this subject a bit more before I respond," he said.

"While you are thinking, why don't you take another look at the Sermon on the Mount, Matthew 5 and 6," Lassere said. He gave Dietrich a wry smile. "I'm sure you must have read those chapters before."

Dietrich raised his eyebrows. "Yes, I have," he softly responded. "But perhaps I have not read them closely enough."

By the time Dietrich left Union at the end of that academic

year, he had gained a new appreciation for "American" theology, which centered around a mixture of social consciousness and practical church work. He had also gained a new appreciation for the diversity of American Christianity through his regular attendance at Abyssinian Baptist Church. The Harlem church gave him a sense of freedom in worship that he had never experienced in his own country. He didn't feel uncomfortable being the only white man in attendance.

But more than anything, Dietrich had found his traditional Lutheranism shaken to the core by the "peace gospel" that Jean Lassere explained to him in the weeks following their confrontation. He could not help but see it everywhere in Scripture now—especially in the Sermon on the Mount, which he was examining anew. He gradually began to see that if the Church were to stand against nationalism and its inevitable wars, the Church could no longer depend on the state as much as in the past. The Church had to be an independent, moral agent, holding forth the Word of God against every creed and institution of humankind—and obeying the Word of God above all. In other words, the Church had to become a threat to the ruling powers by exhibiting a radical peacefulness.

As he thought about it more, Dietrich realized that a "peace gospel" forced the Church to be revolutionary in a way that he had always vaguely envisioned it to be.

But as he returned to Germany, he was not sure if he was ready to be a part of such a revolutionary church. At least not yet.

seven

Lone Voices

Dietrich was cued by the technician on the other side of the glass and began to read his speech into the microphone. It was a speech about the youth of Germany, who were allowing themselves to become tools of the Nazi party. He was two-thirds of the way into his speech when he said these words:

> *When a leader allows himself to succumb to the wishes of those he leads, of those who will always seek to turn him into their idol, the image of the leader will gradually become the image of the "mis-leader".... This is the leader who makes an idol of himself and his office, and who thus mocks God.*[1]

Suddenly he saw the technician waving at him, and he stopped reading.

"You have been cut off," the technician said over the

intercom. "We have lost our ability to broadcast."

"What do you mean?" Dietrich asked sharply.

"It seems to have happened from the outside. But hopefully it is only momentary."

"Who has done this?" Dietrich shot back, a bit more aggressively than he meant to sound.

Just then two gray-suited men sporting the red swastika armbands of the now-ruling National Socialist Party entered the recording studio and said something to the technician that Dietrich could not make out. The technician immediately left with them.

Dietrich, now alone in the studio, folded his papers and sat down to wait. This sort of incident was becoming commonplace in the Germany of 1933. The speed at which his country had fallen into the grip of Fascism was difficult for Dietrich to understand. Too often he could only watch as previously unthinkable things happened.

Upon returning from America in 1930, Dietrich had plunged himself into all sorts of activities. He became a lecturer at the University of Berlin and used the opportunity to refine into more understandable form some of his thoughts about the Church. Having paid a visit to the eminent theologian Karl Barth almost immediately upon his return, his enthusiasm for Barth's criticism of liberal theology was rejuvenated.

It had become clear to him that liberalism tended to lock Scripture into its historical context and emphasize the human aspect of the Church, rather than its divine sanction and origin. Barth countered this by defending the objective nature of revelation. In other words, he said that the Word of God existed eternally as an objective judge of mankind's actions. According to Barth, ethical standards did not change with the winds of time and circumstance, and it was not for man to judge their absolute relevance. God was God, and man was man. For Barth, liberalism confused the absolute separation between the two. And in doing this, it created people who were religious without being righteous.

But Dietrich had been influenced by liberalism too strongly in his student days for him to give it up entirely. He believed that history and human initiative shaped the way the Word of God was understood and that the Church had to adjust sometimes to make itself relevant to its own time period. He wanted to bridge the gap between Barth and the liberal theologians, but the ways he wanted to do this were still unacceptable to both sides. He was usually too dogmatic for the liberals and too socially minded for Barth. From Dietrich's point of view, though, he was only seeking the truth. And if seeking the truth caused him to exist as a party of one, well, then he was ready for that. After all, he was also a spiritual heir of Martin Luther.

Dietrich's attitude made him anathema to most of his older colleagues at the university. The students, however, were intrigued by his independent thinking and attended his lectures in droves. They liked to hear him criticize the old theology. But Dietrich sensed that the younger generation was looking for more than just his radical ideas about the nature of the Church in the modern world. They seemed to be looking, in a broader sense, for relevance, authority, and meaning in their lives. Most of the students had come of age under the Weimar Republic, a weak governing structure that had done little to restore Germany's prestige and honor. The 1920s in Germany had been a time of officially endorsed religious indifference, and most of the postwar generation was more than willing to rebel against this state of affairs. Most of them were ready to find something—anything—to believe in.

So Dietrich, despite being attracted by the security of a university post, could not shake his feelings of unease about the limits of such a position. Sometimes, he wondered whether his lectures were really being understood, or whether they were being used as propaganda against the authorities, which was not his intention at all. He had little contact with his students outside of the lecture hall, and he had no sense of what their lives were like. Being a pastor in Barcelona had made him concerned about the everyday struggles of ordinary people. He had discovered the rewards of personally involving himself in the lives of others, and now he missed such a challenge.

Consequently, in November of 1931, when Dietrich became an ordained minister in the German Lutheran Church, he enthusiastically took on a slate of practical ministry duties in addition to his lecturing. The first thing he did was to accept the task of leading a confirmation class for a group of young teenaged boys in one of the poorest and roughest sections of Berlin, a section of the city called Wedding. He was eager to have his abilities challenged and his perspective widened. Indeed, part of the reason he took the position was that nobody else wanted it.

Dietrich's first day at Wedding was a revelation. As he walked to the school building with the old pastor whom he was replacing, the white-haired man's hands shook as he told Dietrich about the impossibility of the task at hand.

"These ruffians are absolutely without manners and morals," the pastor said, shaking his head. "It would be a miracle if they were ever confirmed into the church. I'm not sure the church would be any better off for having them, either."

"I have some experience with hard cases," Dietrich said, thinking back to his days in Barcelona.

"Oh, but these children have never known any type of structure in their lives. You try to teach them the simplest thing, and they mock you to no end. The little devils don't even flinch when you make threats. They have no concept of what authority means."

"I'm sure it's not *that* bad," Dietrich said, smiling.

"You will see; you will see."

As the two men approached the building, they could hear the confirmation students before they could see them. It sounded like a riot was going on inside. Then, as they entered the building and began to climb the stairs to the third-floor classroom, the boys looked over the banisters at them and began to howl and pelt them with chalk and erasers. Dietrich covered his head but kept on climbing.

At the top, Dietrich and the pastor had to force their way into the classroom through the throng of twenty or so wild-eyed boys. The older man went to the front of the room and announced above the din that their new teacher had arrived.

"His name is Herr Bonhoeffer!" he shouted.

Immediately the boys began to shout, "Bon! Bon! Bon! Bon!" The pastor threw up his hands and rushed out of the room, leaving Dietrich to handle the situation on his own.

At first Dietrich did nothing. He simply leaned back against the chalkboard and watched the chaos. Everything was exactly as the pastor had described. Boys were wrestling on the floor and laughing at each other's jokes, oblivious to the figure of authority in their midst. They were truly like animals that had been released from their cages. After a few minutes, though, the shouting began to die down as the boys started to look querulously at the sturdy young man who did not seem to be perturbed at all by their behavior. This new pastor even seemed mildly amused.

Then Dietrich began to speak very softly. A few boys in the back of the room did not notice this and continued their wrestling and laughing. But those in the front became quiet and tried to make out what Dietrich was saying. Gradually, more and more of them took notice that their instructor was talking to them. He was not yelling, or trying to shout above them, like the previous instructor. Instead, he was talking to them in a calm and measured tone.

Finally, even the boys in the back sat down at their desks and tried to listen to the story that was being told.

"Harlem was quite a place," Dietrich was saying. "If you went into a church there you wouldn't see people sitting on their hands as they do in the German churches. No, the black Christians of Harlem sing at the top of their lungs and say 'Amen' so loudly during the sermon that you can almost see the wind hitting the preacher's face. Then, after the sermon, they start shouting and dancing down the aisles again."

None of the boys had ever seen a black person, and they were riveted in their seats as Dietrich continued to tell them about his Harlem experiences. But when he noticed their attention lagging, he brought his storytelling to a close.

"I want to compliment you on your performance upon my arrival," he said. "It very much reminded me of my times at Abyssinian Baptist Church. Of course, the people there were shouting and carrying on because they loved

God and wanted to praise Him. They were not just making fools of themselves."

Some of the boys hung their heads when Dietrich said this, but others still looked at him with derision on their faces. They weren't going to be cowed into submission by a mere preacher if they could help it. None of the pastors they had ever known had been worth a whit, in their opinions. But even these recalcitrant ones were gradually won over as the weeks passed, and Dietrich showed himself to be someone who deeply cared about their lives. He insisted on a degree of order in the classroom, but he was willing to let them be boisterous as long as their pranks did not verge on disrespect. Expressions of disrespect, though, were virtually nonexistent after the first few weeks. And, wonder of wonders, the boys also made quick progress in their catechism exercises, so that by the end of winter of 1932 most of them had made a confession of faith and were ready for confirmation.

Dietrich preached their confirmation service, and then, to reward them, took the boys to his parents' country home in Friedrichsbrunn, a trip of more than one hundred miles. Most of the boys had never been outside of Berlin, and to them it seemed like they were traveling halfway around the world. Dietrich took the boys hiking in the woods and climbing on some of the cliffs in a nearby valley. He also played soccer with them in the fields.

Although the housekeeper expressed some indignation at being imposed upon by a group of energetic adolescents, at the end of the weekend trip the only serious damage to the estate was a single broken window. To Dietrich, who had grown to love his charges, and to the boys, who had developed into fairly responsible young men, their five months together were worth much more than the expense of one broken window.

During 1932, Dietrich threw himself into preaching, as well. About once a month, he was invited to preach in different churches around Berlin. He liked this more than he liked lecturing because he saw a sermon as a direct message to the heart of a hearer. A well-delivered sermon could change more than just the minds of those in the congregation. It had the potential to change their whole way of life.

The Nazis were growing in popularity, and the challenge for any preacher was to proclaim God's prophetic Word without compromise. Berliners were in the mood to hear sermons that made them feel better about their Fatherland, but they were not always receptive to messages that made them feel bad about their sin. They wanted a religion that made them better Germans, not a religion that forced them to confront their inward need of a Savior. But Dietrich never failed to give them the latter.

On October 4, 1931, he preached at the Harvest Festival in Berlin, using as his text Psalm 63.

At some point in the psalmist's life something quite decisive happened: God came into his life. From that moment his life was changed. I don't mean that he suddenly became good and pious—he may have been that before. But now God Himself had come and had drawn near to him. What made his life remarkable was simply that God was always there with him, and he could no longer get away from God. It completely tore his life apart. We so often hear and say that religion makes people happy and

*harmonious and peaceful and content. Maybe that's
true of religion; but it is not true of God and His
dealings with humankind. It is utterly wrong. This
is what the psalmist discovered. Something had
burst open inside him. He felt as if he were split in
two. A struggle flared up within him, which every
day became more and more heated and terrible. He
experienced hour by hour how his old beliefs were
being torn out of his inner being. He struggled desperately to hold on to them; but God, standing ever
before him, had taken them from him and would
never give them back.*[2]

Shortly afterward, Dietrich himself sought and found a
deeper place in his relationship with God. He spent more
time reading the Bible, especially the Sermon on the Mount,
and his prayer life was growing deeper, too. Dietrich had
never had a sudden and dramatic "conversion" experience
like the ones testified about at the Abyssinian Baptist Church
in Harlem. Yet as he gradually learned how to recognize
God's grace in his life, he endeavored to respond to that
grace with faith. And he took every new step of faith very
seriously.

But now, as darkness descended on Germany's horizon, Dietrich spoke more frequently about the necessity of
knowing God and of giving oneself up to Him. It was a
theme that he would reiterate most fully in his classic book
The Cost of Discipleship several years later, but in reality,
the book began to be written through his sermons of those
pre-Nazi days.

On November 29, 1931, he preached about the twin
necessities of seeking God and submitting to Him in a

personal way. He expounded particularly on the experience of the seeker:

> . . .*[The seeker knows that] he cannot go to God,*
> *but that God must go to him in His inconceivable*
> *grace. He [the seeker] can do nothing else but*
> *watch and wait—enthusiastically, totally taken up,*
> *deaf toward everyone who would make him con-*
> *fused with doubts, blind to every force that comes*
> *between him and. . .God. Only one thing is of*
> *importance to him. He wants to see God; he wants*
> *to hear God; he wants to receive God; he wants to*
> *know God; he wants to serve God. He wants. . .*
> *nothing else like he wants God.*[3]

On February 21, 1932, the annual Day of National Mourning, Dietrich pressed home the theme that a nation's pursuit of strength and glory was not necessarily the concern of the churches, since the gospel revealed a God who saved through suffering, and who received glory only after He had met with derision. It was a message that cut to the heart of the German people's propensity to look for a powerful, charismatic leader in times of trouble. To Dietrich, this propensity showed how much Germany fell short of being a truly Christian nation. He declared:

> *The wondrous theme of the Bible that frightens so*
> *many people is that the only visible sign of God in*
> *the world is the cross. Christ is not carried away*
> *from earth to heaven in glory, but He must go to*
> *the cross. And precisely there, where the cross*
> *stands, the resurrection is near; even there, where*

everyone begins to doubt God, where everyone despairs of God's power, there God is whole, there Christ is active and near. Where the power of darkness does violence to the light of God, there God triumphs and judges the darkness.

Then he applied this idea directly to the lives of the congregation, while adding a warning.

Christ knows that the way for His disciples also does not lead gloriously and safely directly into heaven, but that they also must go through the darkness, through the cross. Also, they must struggle, because the first sign of the nearness of Christ is that His enemies become great—that the power of temptation, of apostasy, of unfaithfulness, becomes strong. His congregation is led right up to the abyss of confusion about God. His enemies are concealed behind the name of Christ, and now under the appearance of Christlikeness they would entice us away from Him.[4]

These powerful and insightful sermons were preached on the eve of Hitler's ascent, but the words were not taken to heart. Rather, Dietrich was continually being called a radical when, to his mind, he was merely trying to convey the Word of God as purely as he could. Then again, perhaps that was the most radical thing about him.

Dietrich's last major activity of these pre-Hitler days was his work in the ecumenical movement. He had always been able to pick up foreign languages easily, and this facility, combined with his superb theological training, made him useful within an international movement that sought to strengthen relationships between Protestant churches in different lands.

The ecumenical movement in Europe had been created after the Great War to promote the healing of relationships between wartime combatants. It tried to do this by establishing dialogue between the churches in the various countries. Dietrich was attracted to the movement because of the idealism at its core, but he also was convinced early on that the movement could perform a "prophetic" role by calling attention to dangerous tendencies within autonomous and independent national churches. These dangerous tendencies could then be halted or lessened through international pressure. But this could only happen—and here Dietrich stood almost entirely alone in his perceptivity—if the ecumenical movement operated from a fairly clear and strong theological base.

Dietrich was encouraged by a conference of German and French ministers in July of 1932, and that went a long way toward establishing peace and understanding between the two camps. When Dietrich was allowed to speak at the conference, he made the point that the rise of Nazi extremism was partly the fault of those nations that had isolated Germany after the war. He made this risky statement in the interests of honest dialogue, and he was heartened when his rebuke was met with sympathy. All of the participants agreed to work for a stronger peace between the two, often acrimonious, neighboring states.

Still, that single conference, with its atmosphere of submission to biblical principles of unity, was an exception to the rule. Too often Dietrich found that ecumenical

conferences were loath to do the hard work of real recon-
ciliation, demonstrating again their unwillingness to work
towards a biblical foundation for their activities.

In August of 1932, Dietrich stood up at a conference in
Czechoslovakia and declared, to the astonishment of the
other representatives, that the ecumenical movement "had
no theology."[5] To him, this pointed to a lack of spiritual
depth in the movement. He believed that if it were not sol-
idly based on an understandable biblical foundation, the
movement was vulnerable to changes in the political and
diplomatic climate of Europe. Moreover, if the ecumenical
movement wanted to make real progress in its mission, its
representatives would have to be willing to answer criticism from their home countries. They would have to be
willing to be seen sometimes as "unpatriotic." Without a
strong theological framework to justify their work, it
would be unlikely that they would have the spiritual
authority to carry on in spite of such criticism.

The other two points that Dietrich made at the August
conference flowed out of the first one. He went on to attack
those in the movement who were trying to defend certain
dangerous ideas. Two German theologians named Hirsch
and Althous had spoken in ecumenical gatherings about
something called "orders of creation." According to this
concept, some peoples and races were naturally superior
to others. Everything that Hirsch and Althous said was
cloaked in theological language, but Dietrich immediately
recognized the idea for the poisonous doctrine that it was.

Sadly, the willingness of ecumenicals to listen to such
notions betrayed a fatal weakness at their core.

Lastly, Dietrich criticized the movement for the way
its leadership liked to sit around and discuss abstract ideas

71

and pass meaningless resolutions that had no moral force behind them. He declared that the movement liked to do the easy things while putting off the hard job of strengthening the spiritual quality and moral fiber of Christianity in Europe. Dietrich felt that this necessary kind of maturity could only be gained though confession, repentance, and forgiveness. But for some reason, the ecumenical movement did not like to talk about such fundamental principles.

Dietrich never really gave up on the ecumenical movement, despite its limitations. He saw it as performing an essential function within the church at large, but he was never able to give himself completely to a movement that seemed to have deep misunderstandings about what the Church was all about. Except for a few remarkable occasions, like the Fano Conference of 1938, the ecumenical movement would never rise to the prophetic stature that Dietrich envisioned.

The failure of the ecumenical movement was made all the more tragic in 1931 and 1932, when Europe urgently needed an organization to put pressure on the churches in Germany. As racism erupted in the form of scattered violence against Jews, and as the Nazis won 38 percent of the parliament in 1932, the German Christian churches largely stood by, even applauding many of the developments. To Dietrich, it was inexcusable that even the Church would put its desire for a strong and powerful nation above the welfare of individuals within that nation.

And by the time the ecumenical movement girded itself for action against the German churches who had accepted Nazism, it was too late. Their mission was a lost cause. The influence that they might have exerted had been eroded by their unwillingness to squarely face the facts. Evil was on the rampage, and no one was resisting it.

Lone voices like Bonhoeffer's would continue to speak out and fill the prophet's role, but as shown by the cutting off of Dietrich's radio speech on February 1, 1933, lone voices had no power against the omnipresent power and terror of the emerging regime. Indeed, lone voices in Germany would increasingly find themselves to be very much alone.

eight

The Year of Decision

Unknown to Dietrich, this would be Germany's year of decision. Afterward, the die was cast for everything that would follow.

At noon on January 30, with the National Socialists holding a majority in parliament, General Hindenburg, who was the last remaining symbol of Germany's pre—Great War glory days, called upon Adolf Hitler to become Reich Chancellor.

Eberhard Bethge, Dietrich's friend and biographer, has described in dramatic terms how this ascension split the Church in Germany. Quoting two prominent members of both sides, Bethge writes:

A forest of swastika flags surrounded the altar of Magdeburg Cathedral. Similar scenes in other churches were explained from the pulpit in much the same words as those used by Dean Martin at Magdeburg:

*In short, it [the swastika] has come to be the
symbol of German hope. Whoever reviles this symbol of ours is reviling our Germany. The swastika
flags round the altar radiate hope—hope that the
day is at last about to dawn.*

The first sermon given by Bonhoeffer in the Dreilfaltig-
keitskirche in Berlin after Hitler's seizure of power used
different words:

*The Church has only one altar, the altar of the
Almighty. . .before which all creatures must kneel. . . .
He who seeks anything other than this must keep
away; he cannot join us in the house of God. . . .
The Church has only one pulpit, and from that pulpit faith in God will be preached, and no other faith,
and no other will than the will of God, however
well-intentioned.*[1]

As Dietrich read the morning newspapers over the next
few months, a new travesty appeared in the headlines almost weekly. Hitler passed a series of laws that spring
that made it impossible for his power to be challenged. The
first one (with the long and ironic name "The Reich
President's Edict for the Protection of People and State")
took away all rights that in the United States are guaran-
teed by the First Amendment: the freedoms of speech,
assembly, and the press. The "Treachery Law" declared
that anyone who opposed the Nazi party was a traitor to the
country. The "Enabling Act" dissolved the authority of parliament and suspended the German constitution. Finally, the
"Aryan Clause" set Jews apart as a separate group within the

country, taking away almost every single one of their rights as German citizens. Five years later, this last law would see its logical culmination on November 9, 1938, a date that came to be called *Kristallnacht,* meaning "night of broken glass." On that night of rampaging, Jewish places of business were destroyed, and most of the synagogues in Berlin were burned down.

Incredibly, most Germans, even within the churches, thought that these laws were good for Germany, and that they were the heralds of a new and glorious chapter in their nation's history. They saw the Weimar Republic of the last fifteen years as a failed experiment in democracy, and they were eager for order and discipline. All of these laws would last until 1945, and along the way, they would seal the fate of dissidents like Dietrich who opposed them.

In the spring of 1933, those in the German Lutheran Church who sided with the Nazis began to try to gain control over the National Church as a whole. These politically minded churchmen took advantage of the escalating anti-Semitism throughout the country to skillfully combine nationalism with a religious fervor for "purity" in the churches. They hailed the rise of Hitler as the ascent of a new spiritual leader who would restore Germany's cultural greatness and initiate a new thousand-year reign of Aryan Christianity throughout Europe. According to the rhetoric, this Christianity would be pure because Jews and other "weaker races" would be excluded from it.

When these "German Christians" (as they called themselves) rapidly gained influence within the state apparatus through their courting of Hitler, they also sought to apply the new laws, including the Aryan Clause, to the government of the churches. With this move, a resistance movement began to form. Dietrich sided with the resisters immediately and was the first to speak out against the application of the Aryan Clause.

At a discussion group of pastors in April, he gave an address entitled "The Church and the Jewish Question" in which he criticized the Nazis for overreaching their prerogatives in regard to the churches. It was a bold warning to the new regime and a declaration that the Church of Christ stood in closer relationship to God's authority than the state's. In many ways, even though most of the dissidents were more ambivalent about the Jewish situation than Dietrich, it was an energizing moment for the emerging resistance movement.

Dietrich declared that it was possible for the state to exercise too much law and order:

That means that the state develops its power to such an extent that it deprives Christian preaching and Christian faith. . .of their rights— a grotesque situation, as the state only receives its peculiar rights from this proclamation and from this faith, and enthrones itself by means of them. The Church must reject this encroachment of the order of the state and of the limitations of its action. The state which endangers the Christian proclamation negates itself.

Then he went on to lay out the only possible responses of the churches to this encroachment of state authority.

All this means that there are three possible

77

*ways in which the Church can act toward the
state: In the first place. . .it can ask the state
whether its actions are legitimate and in accor-
dance with its character as a state, i.e., it can
throw the state back on its responsibilities.
Second, it can aid the victims of state action. The
Church has an unconditional obligation to the
victims of any ordering of society, even if they do
not belong to the Christian community—"Do
good to all people". . .The third possibility is not
just to bandage the victims under the wheel, but
to jam a spoke in the wheel itself. Such action
would be direct political action.*[2]

Unbeknownst to Dietrich at this time, this progression of options was to be the actual evolution of his resistance activities over the next ten years: dialogue, assistance to the victims, and direct revolutionary action. Considered this way, his address was an unconsciously prophetic statement.

In the early months of the resistance (or the Confessing movement, as it would come to be known), Dietrich worked energetically with others to make a break from the German National Church. In August, he helped to write the "Bethel Confession," which was the first formal statement of opposition to the new Reich Church policies.

The confession was a theological statement of disagreement. In essence, the dissenters at Bethel disagreed primarily with the contention of the German Christians that Israel had been *replaced* by Germany as God's chosen nation. This was a clear heresy from the dissenters' point of view and had to be met with solid theological opposition.

Thus, the confession stated, "God chose Israel from

among all the nations of the earth to be His people," not because they were "preeminent," but only by "the power of His Word and for the sake of His lovingkindness." The Jews had rejected Christ because they had wanted a "national Messiah, who would bring them political freedom and the rule of the world," but "Jesus Christ was not this, and did not do this."

Instead, the "barrier between Jew and Gentile [was] broken down by the crucifixion and resurrection of Jesus Christ. . .[and] the place of the Old Testament people of the covenant was not taken by another nation, but by the Christian Church, called out of and living among all nations."

Yet (the confession continued), God had kept faith with Israel by promising to retain a remnant for Himself, as fully explained in Romans 9–11. The church inherited a responsibility to reach out to the Jews and baptize them into this new body, this new chosen people, not identified by blood or race, but only "by the Holy Spirit and baptism." Therefore, the confession declared, "We oppose the attempt to deprive the German Evangelical Church of its [calling] by the attempt to change it into a national church of Christians of Aryan descent."[3]

Then in early September, Dietrich helped one of Germany's most prominent pastors, Martin Niemöller, to set up the Pastor's Emergency League, an organization devoted primarily to helping Lutheran ministers who were of Jewish descent. Still, these actions were not enough to halt the growing strength of the German Christians. The Reich (or National Socialist) Church was successful on almost every front in consolidating its power, while the resistance remained weak and relatively scattered.

This state of affairs became painfully clear on September 5 and 6, when a prominent meeting of ministers was held in Berlin in which most of the new Reich Church leaders wore brown, paramilitary uniforms. Resolutions were passed at this meeting that barred the hiring of ministers throughout the National Church who did not give "unconditional support to the National Socialist State." Any future hiring of "non-Aryans" was also forbidden. This meeting was later dubbed "The Brown Synod," in reference to the uniforms worn by the participants.

Because of these conditions, Dietrich decided to take a hiatus from events in Germany and accept pastoral positions at two small German-speaking churches in London, England. But his decision to leave was made on the spur of the moment, and it would soon plague his conscience, making his hiatus not entirely peaceful.

nine

London

The gray skies, punctuated only by occasional rays of sunshine, reflected Dietrich's mood about the situation in Germany. He was trying to remain optimistic, but increasingly he felt alone, and lonely, in his opposition to Nazism in general, and the new Reich Church in particular. Most of the other German church leaders who opposed Nazism spoke primarily of reform, as if a National Socialist Church could still be a fully Christian church. But Dietrich could not think like this. He thought that heresy was not something to be reformed. It had to be rejected outright.

Many other intellectuals and scientists, such as the theologian Paul Tillich and the physicist Albert Einstein, had already seen the writing on the wall and had immigrated to America. Dietrich saw things just as clearly but wavered in his reaction. He felt a strong responsibility to keep struggling against the new church establishment, and to keep proclaiming the biblical idea of the Church. But he also saw this as a doomed struggle unless more leaders rose above equivocation and compromise. There was no guarantee that this would ever happen.

Other questions related to his presence in London also plagued him. Ostensibly, he was there to gain international support for the resistance and to pastor two German congregations on the outskirts of London. Both were noble tasks. As for as the latter, he welcomed his pastorates as a relief from the pressures of political activity and from the oppressive intellectual atmosphere of the university. He also loved being a pastor and helping ordinary people grow closer to God.

But couldn't his acceptance of a post outside the borders of Germany also signal a desire to simply escape from a threatening situation? Did he fear the possible consequences that his resistance activities might bring, more than he feared the failure of the resistance itself? Already parish pastors in Germany were being arrested and detained on charges of disloyalty to the new regime. By moving to England, did Dietrich merely want to maintain his freedom?

Since he could not be sure of his motives, this confusion made it difficult for him to concentrate on his new duties, which were plentiful.

First, there was the obligation of preaching to two congregations each week. One (St. Paul's) was made up of professionals and embassy workers. The other (Sydenham) consisted of tradesmen and their families. He tried to keep this difference in mind as he prepared his sermons, but he was nevertheless sure that much of his theology simply went over the heads of the Sydenham folks.

To lessen the gap, he tried to fill his messages with illustrations drawn from the experiences and concerns of working people. One Sunday, in order to make a point about the nearness of God's salvation, he referred to a recent mining disaster in Wales that had been heavily reported in the papers. Some miners had been trapped under rubble for such a long time that they had almost given up hope. But just as they were beginning to resign themselves to death, they heard their rescuers breaking through the rubble. The trapped miners were instantly energized by hope and were eventually rescued. Dietrich's text for the day was Luke 21:28: "And when these things begin to come to pass, then look up, and lift up your heads; for your redemption draweth nigh."[1]

As far as the other duty, that of gaining outside support for the resistance movement, Dietrich early on made the acquaintance of one of the most prominent leaders of the Anglican Church in Great Britain, Bishop George Bell of Chichester. Bishop Bell was a short and sturdy man with a strong face and white hair that flowed back from a high forehead. He was a scholar and a diplomat, but he was also a friendly and plainspoken host to Dietrich. Since Dietrich was not yet thirty years old, he quite naturally looked up to the bishop as a father figure.

When they were able to get together, Dietrich and Bishop Bell would usually walk the manicured lawns of the parsonage at Chichester and discuss the rapidly developing crisis in Dietrich's home country. Dietrich was able to confess his personal doubts and fears to the bishop, while Bell was willing and eager to fulfill the role of a pastor to the young minister.

On one occasion in late November 1933, they both stood at the window of Bell's booklined study and looked out at the rain that had disallowed their morning stroll. A member of the bishop's staff had brought in hot tea and scones, but neither of the men felt like eating or drinking right away. Both were preoccupied with thinking about the recent persecution of pastors in Germany.

"I feel like my mind is split in two, George," Dietrich said. "There are good reasons for me to be here in London, but I cannot feel at home here—no matter how nicely I am treated."

"That's because you are beginning to feel like an exile," the bishop answered softly.

"An exile? But I have been here less than a month."

"Yes, but in times like these each day stretches out into what seems like a month. We are more conscious of time because of the unpredictability of events."

Dietrich sighed. "I suppose that is true. But still, I feel like I have selfishly separated myself from the struggle. I have trouble shaking the notion that I'm nothing more than a coward in hiding."

"Dietrich," Bishop Bell said, putting a fatherly hand on his shoulder, "I believe that you are exactly where God wants you to be right now. No one else could do what you are doing. I would urge you not to let guilt prevent you from making the most of your opportunities. Otherwise, you will truly be found guilty."

Neither knew what to say next, so they both looked out the window in silence. The rain was decreasing to a light sprinkle, and the overcast sky seemed to be brightening a bit. The surrounding gardens also seemed to glow in phosphorescent shades of green.

"All my thoughts of late have revolved around the question of who Jesus Christ is for us today," Dietrich said, breaking the silence.

"What do you mean?" Bishop Bell asked.

"I mean that even in the evangelical Church we tend to think of Jesus' commands as historical artifacts, as sayings to be admired rather than obeyed without question. Most importantly, we fail to recognize them as commands at the precise moment at which the command is applicable. If we miss that moment, we've also missed our opportunity to obey that command. It has become almost second nature for us as a Church to put things off, to study things to death, and then analyze the results of our indecision and disobedience. And all along we think that God is forgiving us. We are operating under a fallacy of cheap grace, thinking that we can bargain with God about our response."

"I understand what you are saying," Bishop Bell responded as he poured a cup of tea for both of them. "I see it all the time among the church leaders here in England. They are passive and given to fruitless discussion. But where I think you go too far is in believing that it is always a simple thing to understand the will of God. Isn't it sometimes wise to wait on the Lord—to let Him work through circumstances in order to bring about His own will?"

"I think that we could make use of that luxury if our enemies were also waiting," Dietrich said, "but they are not. They are plotting further evils on a daily basis, and they are most certainly rejoicing in our apparent impotence.

"Yes, we should avoid all unnecessary rashness," Dietrich continued as he accepted the cup of tea proffered by the bishop, "but we should also act decisively and courageously at times, even when we are only making an educated guess as to the perfect will of God. Besides, in my reading of the Old Testament, I have noticed that the only times God rebuked His prophets were when they wavered and were fearful. They were never rebuked for being reckless in their proclamation of the Word of the Lord."

Bishop Bell blew softly across the surface of his steaming tea. His eyes were smiling in the peculiar way in which an Englishman's eyes can express a smile. After taking a sip, he said, "Perhaps the heaviness you feel comes from the weight of the prophet's mantle across your shoulders?"

Dietrich blew across his own tea. "I do not aspire to the prophet's role," he said. "I only want to be a good disciple of Jesus Christ."

The bishop sighed. "Yes, but the shame nowadays is that, even in the Church, anyone who makes such a statement is laughed at and treated as a fool. Insincerity is automatically assumed."

Dietrich smiled and searched the bishop's face.

"Do you think I am a fool, George?"

"Of course I do," the bishop said, smiling back. "But we could use many more fools like you."

ten

Reich Church

A huge crowd of German Christians had assembled at the Sports Palace in Berlin. The gathering was meant to be a giant rally to celebrate the union between the German Protestant churches and the new regime of Adolf Hitler. Most of the assembled would agree that this was a momentous time in the history of the Church. They believed that such a union would help to restore the waning prestige of the Church and also mobilize and inspire the youth of Germany toward a new and exhilarating level of Christian militancy. But as in the case of a hasty marriage between two individuals who are ill suited to one another, the implications of the union had not been fully considered.

These implications would be clarified in short order by a Dr. Krause, a senior Nazi official, who gave the opening speech. At a podium draped with a red swastika flag, Krause spoke clearly into the microphone, declaring that everything tainted by Judaism had to be purged from the "new Christian consciousness." He even went so far as to encourage the removal of long-standing Jewish Christians from the membership rolls of the churches. He called for a "liberation from the Old Testament with its Jewish money morality and from these stories of cattle-dealers and pimps," which, in effect, was an announcement that a strict anti-Semitism was to be enforced as the official policy of the German churches. It was also implied that to diverge from this policy would bring governmental discipline upon the offending congregation.[1]

Many who sat in the audience that day were uncomfortable at Krause's words, but their discomfort was not so keen as to spur them to protest.

When Dietrich heard about the Sports Palace demonstration, he was not surprised. It merely made things plainer, more out in the open. Combined with other travesties, the latest revelation prompted Dietrich and the other German pastors in England to get together and write their own letter of protest, outlining the theological heresies of the Reich Church government. Their letter stated that the German churches outside of Germany would not hesitate to break from the "Mother Church" if there were any further official statements that lessened the status of the Old Testament within the canon of Scripture, or that implied that Jews were not worthy of salvation.

It was a strong letter, and they did not have to wait long for a response.

In early February of 1934, Bishop Theodor Heckel, one of the leaders of the Reich Church in Germany, visited England to set the rebellious pastors straight. The meeting between the bishop and the ministers took place at St. George's Church in London. The bishop and his stern-looking entourage sat at one long table, and the pastors sat at another. Flickering candles lighted the ancient conference room, which had not yet been wired for electricity. There was electricity in the air, though, as Bishop Heckel began the formal discussion.

"I have three issues that I would like to address," the thin-lipped man began. "First, the Reich Church is endeavoring to become much more tightly organized so that all of its actions can be carried out with the utmost efficiency. Even as we speak, clear lines of authority are being authorized in Berlin, and the whole church will be expected to follow them. Second, our Führer has decided that Protestant unity is the most important religious issue of the day. Therefore, he is willing to compromise on certain matters, even the Aryan Clause, in order to promote that unity."

Heckel raised his eyes to see whether this second point had caused any reaction among the pastors. When he saw that there was none—the pastors recognized it immediately as a ploy—he resumed. "And third, most of the opposition to the new Church government has already been disciplined and brought back into line. We found that most of these cases involved men who were mentally unbalanced and somewhat fatigued in their ministries."

At this Dietrich rolled his eyes in disgust.

Undeterred, the bishop continued. "We now think that it is time for the best thinkers in the Evangelical Church to spend their energies articulating and refining the policies of the Church, so that they will be widely understood among the congregations, both in Germany and abroad."

Heckel sat up straight in his chair and asked, "Any questions?"

Without hesitation, Dietrich spoke up. "Why is it, Bishop Heckel," he began, "that all the talk coming out of

Berlin has to do with consolidating power and reorganizing lines of authority, as if we were running a factory system? Why is there never any thought given to theological matters? It seems like freedom of speech regarding the Old Testament and the historic confessions of the church has also been done away with."

Heckel considered the young firebrand carefully.

"We German pastors in England are not willing to be party to heresy," Dietrich continued. "We would rather split away than risk our salvation."

"Is this how all of you feel?" Heckel asked the group when Dietrich had finished. And when all of the pastors expressed the same concerns as Dietrich, Heckel went into a lengthy, tedious, and technical discussion of how things were now to be done in the Reich Church, as if Dietrich had not even spoken, and this was just a regular meeting between working partners.

None of what he said directly answered the pastors' concerns about theological correctness. But when Heckel left for Berlin the next evening to report his failure, he directed one of his aides to make a detailed account of Dietrich's "rebellious" behavior, and to enter it into the official record. If he had a chance to squash the volatile upstart some time in the future, he wanted to have some ammunition at the ready.

Dietrich had no idea how worthwhile the meeting with Heckel had been, but he tried to keep the pressure on Berlin by writing letters to Barth, Niem ller, and others. And for the rest of his time in England, he met frequently with Bishop Bell, discussing the frequent abuses of authority that were occurring in Berlin. It was through Dietrich that the bishop gained an absolute distrust of Hitler. In fact,

Bishop Bell became one of the German leader's earliest, and loudest, critics outside of Germany. Dietrich regularly heard of German pastors who were giving in to the Nazi policies, but he was able to find encouragement in the bishop's steadfast support.

Often the two men would not discuss events in Germany at all, choosing instead to spend their times together listening to music or talking about literature. It was a brief reprieve from the unsettling nature of the times. Dietrich's friendship with the older man was one of the few refreshments to his spirit during those days when his home country was spiraling toward an apocalypse.

Despite Dietrich's worries about the breakdown of the opposition in Germany, the core group of dissenters remained fairly strong. There was growing sentiment for breaking all ties with the Reich Church, especially as Hitler grew more and more powerful. This feeling culminated in one of the most important documents in the history of Christendom, the Barmen Declaration.

Like the American Declaration of Independence, the Barmen Declaration, drafted by Karl Barth and signed by most of the leaders of the resistance in late May of 1934, provided a list of grievances against the Mother Country, or the Mother Church in this case. It boldly denounced the heresies of the Reich Church and pledged sole allegiance to Christ as Lord of His Church. It rejected the following:

> *The false doctrine that the Church. . .could and should, over and above God's one Word, acknowledge other events, powers, images, and truths as divine revelation. . . .*

The false doctrine that the form of her [the Church's] order and mission can be left to the discretion of the Church or to the ideological and political views that happen to prevail. . .or that she can set up, or allow herself to be given, special leaders with sovereign powers. . . .[2]

Dietrich himself was not at the Barmen Conference as he was busy with his duties in London at the time. But the declaration was, at least in small part, the product of his constant pushing and prodding for the resistance to make a definitive stand. Much of the wording had come out of his discussions and correspondence with Barth. The need for the Church to remain true to its Reformation principles was one area where he and the older theologian had absolutely no disagreement.

But Dietrich knew that many within the newly created "Confessing Church" still considered themselves to be reformers rather than revolutionaries. Most still felt a strong sentimental attraction to the German National Church and believed that their act of separation was merely temporary. Once the more antagonistic elements were purged, many would be happy to return to the fold, even if that fold were still draped with a Nazi flag.

Dietrich, of course, hoped the break would be much more decisive. To him, the Reich Church was no church at all. In his opinion, a resistance that did not see this was necessarily a weak resistance.

In the months following the Barmen Declaration, the only response of the Reich Church to the rebellion was to strengthen its allegiance to Hitler and to increase its persecution of those who failed to submit. This became especially ominous in August when President Hindenburg died, and Hitler had himself declared "Führer and Reich Chancellor of the German Republic," a combination of the two highest positions in Germany. There now remained no one in Germany who was capable of providing a balance to Hitler's power. He was, from that summer on, a dictator with absolute authority.

Immediately following his assumption of this authority, Hitler approved the implementation of a "service oath" for all of Germany's pastors and church leaders. This oath required not only a pledge of loyalty to the National Socialist party (a pledge most German pastors had already made) but a promise of personal loyalty to Hitler himself. It read: "I swear before God that I will be true and obedient to the Führer of the German people and state, Adolf Hitler, and I pledge myself to every sacrifice and service on behalf of the German people such as befit an evangelical German."[3]

With this, the apostasy of the new regime was complete.

Dietrich saw that the only place to turn was to the ecumenical movement, which he believed could play a pivotal role by denying the authenticity of the so-called German Christians. Dietrich hoped that acceptance of the Confessing Church by the ecumenical movement would influence and inform other nations' opinions of what was going on. Thus he pushed for an absolute rejection of the Reich Church's claims to be the legitimate representative of Christianity within Germany. For if the ecumenical movement wanted to represent the Christian Church on a worldwide scale, it was imperative first of all that it remain truly Christian and go about its business in a Christian way.

Dietrich expressed these sentiments in an August

letter to the presiding bishop of the ecumenical movement, Bishop Ammundson.

> *We must make it clear—fearful as it is—that the*
> *time is very near when we shall have to decide*
> *between national socialism and Christianity. . . .*
> *It may be fearfully hard and difficult for us all,*
> *but we must get right to the root of things, with*
> *open Christian speaking and no diplomacy. And*
> *in prayer together we will find the way.*[4]

Later that month, the worldwide ecumenical conference in Fano, Denmark, showed its sensitivity to Dietrich's concerns by boldly recognizing the Confessing Church as the most legitimate Protestant church in Germany. This was a dramatic moment in the church struggle, and seemed to betoken a turning of the tide.

Dietrich, who was one of the central speakers at the conference, got the attention of the assembled when he characterized (correctly, in retrospect) the two sides as representing more than just two sides of a theological argument. He characterized them as representing war and peace, with the true church the one that works for peace. Using Psalm 85:8 as his text, he stated that the true church was actually under a "peace commandment":

> *. . .Peace on earth is not a problem [to be*
> *solved], but rather a commandment given at*
> *Christ's coming. There are two ways of reacting to*
> *this command of God: the unconditional, blind*
> *obedience of action, or the hypocritical question*
> *of the serpent: "Yea, hath God said? . . ." This*

question is the mortal enemy of obedience, and therefore the mortal enemy of all real peace. . . . He or she who questions the commandment of God before obeying has already denied Him.

Then, later in the sermon he stated:

How does peace come about? Through a system of political treaties? Through the investment of capital in different countries? Through the big banks, through money? Or through universal peaceful rearmament in order to guarantee peace? Through none of these, for the single reason that in all of them peace is confused with safety. There is no way to peace along the way to safety. For peace must be dared. It is the great venture. It can never be safe. Peace is the opposite of security. To demand guarantees is to mistrust, and this mistrust in turn brings forth war. To look for guarantees is to want to protect oneself. Peace means to give oneself altogether to the law of God, wanting no security, but in faith and obedience laying the destiny of the nations in the hand of Almighty God, not trying to direct it for selfish purposes. Battles are won, not with weapons, but with God. They are won where the way leads to the cross. Which of us can say he or she knows what it might mean for the world if one nation should meet the aggressor, not with weapons in hand, but praying, defenseless, and for that very reason protected by a "bulwark that never fails"?[5]

Dietrich's radical, and somewhat utopian, views helped to galvanize the ecumenical movement in its support of the Confessing Church. This was made clear by events that happened after the Fano Conference. The Nazi government attempted to crack down once again on dissenting churches, but this time they were rebuffed by international and internal pressure that forced the regime to allow some measure of religious freedom. In this atmosphere of international support, the Confessing Church organized itself, creating its own preacher's seminaries, one of which would be led by Dietrich the following year.

Dietrich himself was energized at the Fano Conference by the presence of Jean Lassere, the man who had introduced him to the "peace gospel" at Union Seminary in New York. They spent three days together, talking about old times and lending each other moral support for the tough fight ahead. Dietrich's commitment to the New Testament peace commandments was also strengthened during these days. He realized anew that the Confessing Church could not compromise on this issue. It could not give in to a war-hungry regime.

But soon more moderate voices within the Church, and especially within the ecumenical movement, took over and caused a lessening of pressure upon the Reich Church. Dietrich was disappointed by this refusal to build upon a victory, which fed a growing disillusionment with political measures that Dietrich was experiencing during these years. As it became clear over the following winter that Fano represented the peak of the church resistance and not just a first step toward something greater, Dietrich turned his attention more and more to purely spiritual matters. As expressed in his sermon at Fano, he believed that the conflict within Germany was a spiritual one and that true peace could only come about through prayer and a collective change of heart.

He was also discouraged by how his fellow dissenters failed to understand the true nature of the church conflict. Many of them acted as if Hitler and the leaders of the Reich Church were simply "bad Nazis," and that they, the dissenters themselves, could be "good Nazis" if given the chance. Many of them were also willing to go to war to save the regime, plainly ignoring what Dietrich saw as the plain teaching of the Bible on war and peace. They simply were not radical enough to respond in a Christian way to the crisis at hand. They labeled all courageous actions as extremism, as if extremism were not the exact remedy for an extreme situation.

Dietrich revealed his frustrations in a letter to his Grandmother Tafel in May 1934, writing, "Unfortunately I have hardly any confidence left in the church opposition. I thoroughly dislike their way of going about things, and I really dread the moment when they assume responsibility, and we must once again witness a terrible compromising of Christianity."[6]

To Dietrich, there was only one prominent person in the world who was fulfilling the type of radical peaceful resistance that he idealized—and that was Mahatma Gandhi. All through the 1930s, Dietrich read everything he could by and about the great Indian leader. His friends thought his fascination with such a figure was strange, to say the least. But Dietrich saw Gandhi as a rebuke to Western complacency. While Western Christians were reading their newspapers and fretting impotently about the state of the world, a gentle Hindu from a colonized nation was actually living out the

Sermon on the Mount on a daily basis.

Dating back to his pastorate in Barcelona, Dietrich had periodically tried to get away to India in order to learn how nonviolent resistance and deep spirituality could be combined. It was not that he found anything compelling about formal Hindu doctrines, but he could not help but notice the contrast between the liberal social Christianity of Western Europe and the politically radical, yet thoroughly religious, practices of Gandhi's supporters.

As Dietrich's time in London was coming to an end, he again tried to set up a trip to India. He even got Bishop Bell to write a letter of introduction to Gandhi for him. But the needs of the Confessing Church thwarted this last attempt to make an Indian pilgrimage. His longing to find examples of a relevant, deep, and structured spirituality would have to be satisfied by visits to a few Anglican monasteries in the English countryside. The Confessing Church could not wait for him to develop his ideas any further before he put them into concrete action. He was being called upon to lead one of the new preacher's seminaries where the Church hoped to develop a new kind of Christian leader.

Despite his disappointments, Dietrich resolved to make the most of this opportunity. He wrote to his brother, Karl-Friedrich, in January of that year:

> *The restoration of the Church must surely depend on a new kind of monasticism, having nothing in common with the old but a life of uncompromising adherence to the Sermon on the Mount in imitation of Christ. I believe the time has come to rally men together for this.*[7]

98

eleven

Confessing Church

The site where Dietrich would put into practice his "new kind of monasticism" was a large building on the outskirts of the town of Finkenwalde, near the Baltic coast. The building had formerly been a private high school, but the Nazis preferred institutions that they could easily control, and thus the school had been shut down.

From the outside, the building looked like an oversized house or small hotel. It had a large room for communal dining, a music room that contained two grand pianos, and even a gymnasium. But the accommodations were otherwise fairly spartan, and the rooms were often drafty. It wasn't the perfect place to run a seminary, but it would have to do. The Confessing movement could not afford anything else.

To start a preacher's seminary was a risky proposition. It was not a German tradition for preachers in the Lutheran Church to go to a seminary following their undergraduate work. Usually they simply went on to get an advanced degree in a normal university setting, as Dietrich had done. But with the rise of the Reich Church, and the expulsion of dissenting theologians from the staffs of most universities, any young man who wanted to be a minister and who also opposed the new way of doing things was left without a place to get advanced training.

To their credit, the leaders of the Confessing movement recognized this problem early on and seized the opportunity to create their own training grounds. It was envisioned that the young men who came out of these seminaries after a year of instruction would be firebrands in the movement and unshakeable in their theological purity.

The leaders of the seminaries had to fulfill certain curricular requirements, but otherwise they were free to shape the experience in any way they saw fit. Whether the experiments worked or not usually depended on the quality of the leadership.

One Saturday, Dietrich and the twenty-three new ordinands (or candidates for ordination) of Finkenwalde seminary sat facing each other around a large oaken table. Winds off the not-too-distant sea rattled the windows on one wall of the spacious dining room, and Dietrich had to speak loudly to be heard. Since he wanted to set aside Sundays for outings, recreation, and rest, he had chosen Saturdays for his weekly sermon to the students. Despite the fact that they were in a dining room, it was the only time that Dietrich preached in a formal manner, the other days of the week being filled with practical lessons and lectures.

This particular Saturday, Dietrich decided to encourage the ordinands to fear God above all. After reading Revelation

14:6–13, he focused on verse 7, stating his interpretation of the passage in terse terms.

> . . .*The language is so simple that everyone must understand it: "Fear God, and give glory to him; for the hour of his judgment is come: and worship him that made heaven, and earth, and the sea, and the fountains of waters." That is the first commandment, the entire gospel. "Fear God" — instead of the many things which you fear. Do not fear the coming day, do not fear other people, do not fear power and might, even if they are able to deprive you of property and life; do not fear the great ones of this world; do not even fear yourselves; do not fear sin. All this fear will be the death of you. You are free from all this fear; it isn't there for you. But fear God and Him alone; for He has power over the powers of this world; the whole world must fear Him—He has power to give us life or to destroy us; everything else is a game—only God is in earnest, entirely in earnest. Fear God's earnestness—and give Him the glory. He demands it as the creator of the world, as our creator; He demands it as the reconciler, who made peace between God and man in Christ; He demands it as the Savior, Who will liberate us in the end from all sin and burden. Give glory to Him in His holy gospel— "for the hour of His judgment is come."*

All of the young men around the table had given up promising careers, reputations, and salaries in order to serve the Confessing Church. By their very presence in the drafty house at Finkenwalde, they were testifying that they esteemed the gospel above worldly ambitions. Yet Dietrich knew that many of them were still fearful and tentative in their faith, not sure if the sacrifices were necessary. Thus he encouraged them further:

> *What will God ask about on that day of judgment that we are approaching? At the judgment, God will ask us solely about His everlasting gospel: Did you believe and obey the gospel? He won't ask whether we were Germans or Jews, whether we were Nazis or not, not even whether we belonged to the Confessing Church or not; nor whether we were great and influential and successful, nor whether we have a life's work to show for ourselves, nor whether we were honored by the world or unimportant or insignificant, unsuccessful and unappreciated. All persons shall be asked by God one day whether they could risk submitting to the test of the gospel. The gospel alone shall be our judge.*

Dietrich paused to look around the table. Most of the faces were turned toward him, eager to hear the Word. But some eyes were downcast. Dietrich could not be sure if these despondent ones were even listening, but he was unwilling to compromise the message in order to lighten their hearts. Instead he pressed his point home:

> *The road divides for eternity at the gospel. When we know this, and yet see how the gospel is disregarded among us—both in the world and in*

the church—then we may well become fearful.[1]

Dietrich finished the sermon by exhorting the students to die to everything—selfish desires, unforgiveness, discouragement—that might keep them from living for the gospel. He had high hopes for the group assembled around the table, and he didn't want them to think that merely joining the Confessing Church was enough. They had to be strong and dedicated to be able to make hard decisions in the future. Dietrich knew better than they what was happening to regional pastors who were resisting the increasing number of laws that were directed against dissenters in the churches. He already recognized the possibility that things might get much worse before they got better. The ordinands had to be ready to endure anything, and they could only do that by centering all of their faith, hope, and desire on God alone.

Dietrich's methods for helping the ordinands to reach this place of discipleship included his imposition of a rigorous daily schedule. Drawing on his study and observations of various religious communities, he organized the day around prayer, study, and meditation, making sure that the living conditions remained clean but well short of luxurious. He also tried to maintain the relative seclusion of the group so that they might cultivate a true sense of community.

Not that there was much to do in the surrounding town anyway. Finkenwalde was isolated from the amenities of German culture. The town had been decimated by the loss of local industry, and there was no entertainment to be found in the evenings. Not even a decent restaurant had remained open after the postwar economic downturn. All of the ordinands went through periods when they deeply longed for various comforts of home, whether it was schnitzel, warm, brown bread, a night at the cinema, or even goose-down mattresses in their own private bedrooms. At Finkenwalde, everybody slept together, barracks-style, in a single, large room.

Such a hothouse environment was bound to create certain tensions and even grumbling among the participants. One part of Dietrich's regimen required the ordinands to engage in one half hour of silent meditation upon a single passage of Scripture each morning. None of the young students had ever been taught how to do this, and most found it impossible to concentrate on what they were supposed to do. At university, they had been taught to read the Bible as if it were an academic textbook; to read it in order to find out what God might be saying to them *individually* was a foreign concept.

Most of them reported back that their minds wandered endlessly, and that the half hour was not beneficial. Dietrich continued to encourage them in the practice, telling them of the benefits it had brought to his own devotional life. Yet he occasionally allowed them to meet as a group to discuss the Scripture, and these breaks from the routine seemed to ease any developing discontent.

As the semester progressed, the group of ordinands at Finkenwalde became a tightly knit group, despite the tensions. Dietrich's experimental way of doing things was being talked about throughout the Confessing movement, and eventually a steady stream of visitors began to make its way to the Finkenwalde house to observe the ordinands and to ask questions. This attention caused the ordinands to have a greater sense of purpose. If the outside world was fascinated with them, they reasoned, they must be doing something important. Dietrich tried to accommodate the groups of "seekers," but he found that they hindered his attempt to be totally available to the ordinands themselves. The outsiders were a threat to the sense of community he wanted to encourage, and more and more he tried to ignore them.

Soon Dietrich had an idea for an even more strenuous type of monastic experience. He told the ordinands that he was prepared to remain at Finkenwalde after the end of the academic year in order to lead a smaller group of men into a deeper walk of spiritual devotion and mutual encouragement. Not unexpectedly, there wasn't too much enthusiasm for such a project at first. Most of the ordinands could not wait to get back home. But by the end of the year, a small cluster of students (including Dietrich's future biographer, Eberhard Bethge) had decided to be a part of what Dietrich called "The House of Brethren."

By the summer of 1936, the Finkenwalde seminary had become known as a spiritual boot camp for the advance guard of the Confessing Church. The seminarians' intense resolve to resist all pressures to conform to the Reich Church policies had gained them notoriety among all the German churches. Yet the seminary was, in many ways, under siege.

The first major challenge to the seminary's survival was a lack of funds. Unlike the official state Church, the Confessing movement was not eligible to receive government monies. It was entirely dependent upon freewill gifts and offerings. And with a fairly short membership list, this was a serious dilemma. Providentially, though, Finkenwalde found support from the gentry in the surrounding Pomeranian region. Pomerania had been the site of several intense evangelical revivals in the late 1800s, and many of the landowners were still devout and enthusiastic in their faith. Once they were convinced that the seminary was doing the Lord's work, they were willing to provide generous support. One of these landowning families, the von

Kleist-Retzows, gave money to the seminary but asked that their granddaughters—one of whom was Maria von Wede-meyer, who would one day become Dietrich's fiancée—be catechized there in return.

Another challenge to Dietrich's program at Finkenwalde was the resistance that the ordinands showed to his pacifist principles. Not that he expected them to accept his views completely, but he had hoped to influence more of them toward an appreciation of the New Testament's peace empha-sis. This was not a subject that came up often in the course of Dietrich's lectures, but when it did it met with a surprising amount of scorn. Almost all of the ordinands were perfectly willing to join the army if called and had no scruples about going to war to defend the Fatherland. Like Dietrich, they remembered the shame of losing the Great War to the British, Americans, and especially the French. A certain pall contin-ued to hang over Germany that every patriotic German wanted to dispel, preferably through military victory.

Dietrich, who loved the Fatherland as much as any-body, considered himself to be a patriot. He simply did not understand the thirst for military conquest that seemed to be a part of his countrymen's psyche. He thought of Walter every day and still deemed the loss of his talented older brother a tragic waste. To his mind, war, and especially a war of conquest, always cost more than it was worth. There was always an element of blindness involved in the steps leading up to it, and this blindness created a skewed per-spective on the purposes of God.

Furthermore, as an ecumenist, internationalist, and pacifist—and in contradiction to the reigning ideology—Dietrich considered war itself to be the true enemy of humankind. It was the most purely demonic element in the history of the world. How could something that caused Christians to kill other Christians be judged otherwise, he reasoned. But none of his students saw it that way. Indeed, this was the only issue on which the students were tempted to engage in slight mockery of their teacher.

While Dietrich never showed any lack of respect for the students' antipacifist views, what saddened him almost to the point of despair was the death of several of his students at the front lines in the coming years. When this happened, he took it upon himself to write a lengthy letter to each family that had suffered loss.

The seminary had survived economic and personal crises, but the most serious threat to its survival was the one that eventually would shut it down. This was the Nazi state itself.

As Finkenwalde became known as a bastion of theological and spiritual resistance within the Confessing movement, it gained more attention within the upper realms of the Nazi government. In turn, this caused there to be more attention paid to the Confessing movement generally. On June 9, 1937, a law was passed that made it illegal for anyone to make contributions to any organization connected to the Confessing Church. Five days later, the Gestapo raided the Confessing Church's main offices and rifled its files. Suddenly, Finkenwalde students were being detained by Nazi agents and questioned thoroughly about their activities. Then, on June 23, those in top leadership positions in the movement began to be arrested. Ten weeks later, the doors to Finkenwalde were locked for good, which signaled the end of any real aboveground resistance to Nazi Church policies. It also signaled Dietrich's transition into a new, and eventually fatal, stage in his own personal resistance to the Nazi state.

twelve

The Cost of Discipleship

After Finkenwalde closed, Dietrich found himself in a state of limbo. He had neither a home of his own nor a place of ministry. He kept in touch with his scattered students by sending out circular letters that were filled with encouragement, but these letters also carried an undertone of sadness. There was a sense in them that God's judgment was falling upon Germany, and that nothing would ever be the same again. It was a prophetic sense of things that went against the current since all of Germany seemed to be on an emotional high during those last prewar years. The economy was booming, and Hitler had restored a feeling of national pride.

But Dietrich was also aware of the underside of this "restoration." His sister, Sabine, was married to a Jewish lawyer, Gerhard Leibholz, which allowed Dietrich to stay well informed as to how the situation for Jews in Germany was worsening. In most cases, Jews were already considered "non-persons." This was true for leaders and pastors in the Confessing Church, as well. Two pastors in the Confessing movement who would not remain silent on this issue suffered the consequences of their criticism.

Martin Niemöller, one of the movement's harshest critics of Hitler, was outdoors playing with his young son one morning when Gestapo agents drove up and took him away for questioning. As he had been temporarily detained before, he expected to be back home later that day. Instead, he was imprisoned and did not see his son again until after the war, eight years later.

Schneider, another Confessing pastor, was ordered to leave his home region—the Rhineland—under the accusation that his pastoral activities were "endangering the public safety." In a letter to Hitler himself, Schneider boldly refused to accept his banishment. "I know that I have been called by God to my churches and cannot be separated from them by man," he wrote. After he continued to minister, he was arrested and eventually ended up in the Buchenwald concentration camp, where he was beaten to death in 1939.[1]

In this tense atmosphere, Dietrich was anxious to complete a book he had begun during his time at Finkenwalde, a book that would turn out to be his most popular and enduring work. Most of the writing was done in the town of Kossin, where the von Kleist-Retzow family lived. Dietrich spent many of his evenings at the family home and also had time to carry on a "collective pastorate" in the region with refugees from Finkenwalde. But the book, which he would title *The Cost of Discipleship*, would take up most of his time.

It might seem strange that Dietrich was so consumed with a treatise on the subject of discipleship at a time when politics and international affairs were at the forefront of everyone's mind, both inside and outside the resistance. But his book was much more than a dry monograph on a theological subject. It was a bold call for a new Reformation, and an assessment of the reasons why German Christianity had descended so far toward paganism.

Following the model of the first Protestant Reformation, Dietrich began by calling for the Church to prune away dead accretions and to return to the pure Word of God. This was the prerequisite for any true life to reinhabit the Church. He wrote:

> *Revival of church life always brings in its train a richer understanding of the Scriptures. Behind all the slogans and catchwords of ecclesiastical controversy. . .there arises a more determined quest for Him who is the sole object of it all, for Jesus Christ Himself. What did Jesus mean to say to us? What is His will for us today? . . . The real trouble is that the pure word of Jesus has been overlaid with so much human ballast—burdensome rules and regulations, false hopes and consolations— that it has become extremely difficult to make a genuine decision for Christ.*

Then he entered into the heart of his argument—that Lutheran Germany (or the Germany of Luther) had distorted the truth of justification by faith into an emphasis on what Dietrich called "cheap grace." He defined cheap grace as the following:

> *The grace which amounts to the justification of sin without the justification of the repentant sinner who departs from sin and from whom sin departs.*

*Cheap grace is not the kind of forgiveness of sin
which frees us from the toils of sin. Cheap grace is
the grace we bestow on ourselves. . . .*

*Cheap grace is the preaching of forgiveness with-
out requiring repentance, baptism without church discipline, communion without confession, absolution
without personal confession. Cheap grace is grace
without discipleship, grace without the cross,
grace without Jesus Christ, living and incarnate.*

Dietrich also implied that cheap grace was the grace
offered by most of the churches of liberal Christianity in
Germany. It resulted in too close an identification between
the Church and the world, between the Church and politics,
and between the Church and the nation-state. Hence, it was
also the spiritual key to the church struggle itself, the fault
line upon which the Church had necessarily split. The
implication was that a Church of cheap grace was really no
Church at all. It could never be the body of Christ upon the
earth because it cheapened the whole meaning of the cross
by denying the separation that made it necessary.

The only answer to cheap grace was a renewed call for
what Dietrich called "costly grace." While carefully avoiding the theological pit of equating faith and works too
closely (which would have caused him to repudiate the
very Reformation he was trying to revive), he characterized costly grace as the grace that leads the recipient into a
walk of obedience and true faith.

He would pen a more detailed definition of costly grace:

*. . .The sanctuary of God; it has to be protected
from the world, and not thrown to the dogs. It is*

therefore the living Word, the Word of God, which He speaks as it pleases Him. Costly grace confronts us as a gracious call to follow Jesus, it comes as a word of forgiveness to the broken spirit and the contrite heart. Grace is costly because it compels a person to submit to the yoke of Christ and follow Him; it is grace because Jesus says: "My yoke is easy and my burden is light."

Over and over, Dietrich would stress that real discipleship and real conversion led to the only true freedom and liberation. It was the paradoxical language of the New Testament that he was reflecting. "When Jesus calls a person, He bids him come and die," he wrote.

But he wasn't calling for individual Christians to work up the resolution to deny themselves. That was not the kind of denial that led to a new life. Only when the individual identified with the Christ Who suffered and died, and when he identified with the body of Christ upon earth, the Church, did true self-denial become possible. A church that rejected the necessity of suffering; that rejected the necessity of finding one's identity in Christ alone; that saw the cross as a "scandal" to be ignored in favor of self-righteousness, self-dignity, and self-congratulation, was a purely human institution with no ability to live the divine life. He wrote:

If our Christianity has ceased to be serious about discipleship, if we have watered down the gospel into emotional uplift which makes no costly demands and which fails to distinguish between natural and Christian existence, then we cannot help regarding the cross as an everyday ordinary calam-

112

*ity, as one of the trials and tribulations of life. We
have then forgotten that the cross means rejection
and shame as well as suffering. The psalmist was
lamenting that he was despised and rejected of men,
and that is an essential quality of the suffering of
the cross. But this notion has ceased to be intelligible to a Christianity which can no longer see any
difference between an ordinary human life and a life
committed to Christ. The cross means sharing the
suffering of Christ to the last and to the fullest. Only
a man thus totally committed in discipleship can
experience the meaning of the cross.*

The Church was defined as the assembly of those who
died with Christ. And to have died with Christ was to be
identified with shame and suffering. It was to be the scapegoat that was thrust out into the wild. But it was also the
assembly of those who found new life in Christ. Dietrich
stated that it was not for nothing that the early Church was
a church of martyrs and potential martyrs. They counted
their own earthly lives as nothing compared to the life and
fellowship they had found in Christ. They did not think it
strange that they should suffer the same fate as their Lord.
Instead, they submitted to that fate joyfully and obediently.

Dietrich himself often talked and wrote about his own
potential martyrdom, as in the following passage.

*If we refuse to take up our cross and submit to
suffering and rejection at the hands of men, we
forfeit our fellowship with Christ and have ceased
to follow Him. But if we lose our lives in His service and carry our cross, we shall find our lives*

113

again in the fellowship of the cross with Christ.
The opposite of discipleship is to be ashamed of
Christ and His cross and all the offense which the
cross brings in its train.

In another section of the book, Dietrich looked at the issue of "nonresistance to evil," which was based on the injunction to "turn the other cheek" found in the Sermon on the Mount (Matthew 5:38–42). His commitment to nonviolent resistance was obviously still strong at the time he entered into the conspiracy against Hitler. Some commentators have charged that his willingness to be a part of this conspiracy was a repudiation of the "peace gospel" he had consistently preached, but Dietrich himself did not see it as repudiation but rather as a terrible necessity. He saw the conspiracy as a last resort that had been thrust upon them by a situation in which they had to choose the lesser of two evils.

In 1937, Dietrich was not talking about the evil of the state. He was much more concerned about a situation in which the "established" Church, by identifying itself with the society around it rather than Christ, had actually become the enemy of Christ. Yet, to further complicate matters, it was also one of the enemies that the Christian was commanded to love, even when persecution came from every quarter.

This commandment, that we should love our
enemies and forgo revenge, will grow even more
urgent in the holy struggle which lies before us and
in which we partly have already been engaged for
years. In it love and hate engage in mortal combat.
It is the urgent duty of every Christian soul to
prepare itself for it. The time is coming when the

114

*confession of the living God will incur not only the
hatred and the fury of the world, for on the whole it
has come to that already, but complete ostracism
from "human society," as they call it.*

In the final section of the book, Dietrich spoke about
the need for the Church to cling to a correct image of Christ.
The whole "church struggle" was, for him, a struggle over
the image of Christ. The Reich Church held forth an image
of Christ as a Germanic conqueror, someone who rooted out
his enemies and destroyed them mercilessly. To Dietrich,
this was a pagan image. He instead went back to the
Incarnation, in which God became man in order to reveal
who God actually was. In other words, the Incarnation was
to be the basis of the Church's reformed image of God:

*It is the image of one who enters a world of
sin and death, who takes upon Himself all the
sorrows of humanity, who meekly bears God's
wrath and judgment against sinners, and obeys
His will with unswerving devotion in suffering
and death, the man born to poverty, the friend of
publicans and sinners, the man of sorrows,
rejected of man and forsaken of God. Here is God
made man, here is man in the new image of God.*

Yet the Church that is called to be conformed into this
image cannot do so by human effort. In an attitude of discipleship, it merely submits to God's own work in its midst.

*To be conformed to the image of Christ is not
an ideal to be striven after. It is not as though we*

115

had to imitate Him as well as we could. We cannot
transform ourselves into His image; it is rather
the form of Christ which seeks to be formed in us
(Gal. 4:19), and to be manifested in us. Christ's
work in us is not finished until He has perfected
His own form in us. We must be assimilated to the
form of Christ in its entirety, the form of Christ
incarnate, crucified, and glorified.

Finally, Dietrich reiterated that the Church was the only image of Christ upon earth. It modeled not only the life of Christ, but also the necessary death that was its precedent and result. There was no easy way to God, for He resides behind the cross.

The earthly form of Christ is the form that died
on the cross. The image of God is the image of
Christ crucified. It is to this image that the life of
the disciples must be conformed; in other words,
they must be conformed to His death (Phil. 3:10;
Rom. 6:4). The Christian life is a life of crucifixion
(Gal. 2:19).[2]

As Dietrich weighed his options in the wake of Finkenwalde's demise, he began to allow God to widen his vision. His traditional view of the Christian life was breaking down upon the crucible of events, and he knew that God would be calling him to a path of discipleship that he would not be able to foresee. In writing his book, he had confirmed within himself that he was willing to be obedient to any path, even if that path offended other Christians—and even if that path brought him into perilously close contact with evil.

thirteen

Meeting the Abwehr

D ietrich knocked on the front door of his sister Christine's house. It was late February, and a cold rain pelted his umbrella as he waited for her to respond. Finally she did, apologizing for the delay, and led him into the foyer. There he took off his raincoat and hung it on a tall hat pole.

"I'll go get Hans and the others," she said. "Why don't you wait in the front parlor, Dietrich?"

Sitting on the sofa, he picked up some of the photographs on the table in front of him and examined them. They were of Christine and Hans. Hans was Dietrich's childhood friend who had gone to law school while Dietrich was studying theology. Now he and Christine lived in a spacious house in a fashionable part of Berlin. The expensive furniture and the art on the walls bespoke Hans's success as a lawyer in the Ministry of Justice and as a judge. But from what Dietrich had heard through the grapevine, his brother-in-law

117

was now involved in things that would put all of his hard-earned comfort and security at risk. Dietrich suspected that he had been invited for a visit in order to talk about those very matters.

"Dietrich, I'm so glad to see you," Hans said upon entering the parlor with three older gentlemen in tow. "I would like to introduce you to Admiral Canaris, General Beck, and General Oster."

Dietrich was a bit taken aback by the ranks of the three men, and he became even more suspicious about his reason for being there. His visit did not seem to be a mere social occasion.

"Your brother-in-law has told us quite a lot about you," Admiral Canaris said after he and the others had settled into high-backed chairs. "Your range of experience is very impressive for someone of your age."

"Thank you," Dietrich said. "I like to keep busy." He was starting to feel like he was being interviewed for a job he had never applied for.

"I heard that you spent some time in England and America," General Oster added, and Dietrich nodded. His discomfort was plainly evident on his face.

"I'm sorry, Dietrich," Hans finally said. "You must be confused as to why you are here."

"A little bit," Dietrich admitted.

"Well, I must admit that Christine did not want me to involve you at all," Hans continued. "She tried to tell me that you were only interested in theology, not politics. And that may in fact be true—feel free to tell us if it is—but I also suspect that you may be extremely useful to our cause."

Hans hesitated before going on. "You see, the admiral and the generals comprise the leadership of the Abwehr, an office in which I have only recently taken a position as legal counsel. The Abwehr began in 1934 as the military wing of counterintelligence under the Reich government. Because of the nature of its organization and mission, it enjoys a great deal of freedom and independence from the other branches of Reich security—all of which is advantageous, I might add."

"Advantageous?" Dietrich asked.

"Yes, but we should give you some background first," General Oster said. "Through our information sources, we have obtained hard evidence that Hitler is going to overplay his hand very soon. There are plans drawn up for the invasion of Czechoslovakia and of Poland. We don't think that the German people are psychologically prepared for such military actions. In fact, we believe that they would be outraged, which means that the time might be right for a change of leadership."

"Oh?" Dietrich responded.

"But what you might be even more interested in," Hans broke in, "is that Hitler and his inner circle are going to begin an initiative to rid Germany of every single Jew. As you may know, the Aryan Clause opened the way for persecutions that have already begun—and planning is already underway in the Ministry of Justice to make it impossible for a Jew to make a living in Germany. There are other things going on, too, about which we have only suspicions."

Dietrich caught sight of Christine hovering in the foyer. "Forgive me, gentlemen," he said. "This is all very distressing information, but I'm not sure why you are entrusting me with it."

The military men looked at one another and then back at Dietrich.

"Because we want you to help us to overthrow the

Führer," Admiral Canaris said flatly.

Dietrich was momentarily stunned.

"I would not even be telling you about this, Dietrich," Hans said, "except for the fact that, with your international contacts, you could be an invaluable liaison between us and those nations that will inevitably align themselves against Germany when these military actions are taken. We need someone to convince the leaders of England and America—even if it happens through churchmen—that there are qualified people ready to reconstitute the German government after this criminal regime has been done away with. This is the only way to avert another world war. So, you see, the stakes are very high."

Dietrich could hardly arrange his thoughts as they rushed through his head. In a sense, Christine was right. He was primarily concerned about the church struggle. Yet after five years in which he had seen more defeats than victories, the church struggle was in ruins. There was little else that he could do on that front.

Still, he had never envisioned himself as a political revolutionary. It went against his aristocratic background and genteel upbringing. He also wasn't so sure it didn't go against his theology. It was one thing to foment revolution in the churches against an illegitimate leadership and to go up against other theologians on familiar turf, but it was quite another to rise up against the state itself and try to overthrow a duly elected government.

Admiral Canaris noticed his uneasiness and spoke up. "Reverend Bonhoeffer, I must admit that I am not as passionately concerned about the fate of the Jews as some of the other people in this room. But I see the treatment of that minority as emblematic of a larger chaos within the present government. Since 1933, this regime has shown an increasing arrogance and disrespect for the law and for all the other bases of humane civilization that our families hold dear. You see, I am a German patriot, and as one, I cannot just sit by while a madman destroys the greatest culture this planet has ever produced. Hitler is a reckless, mongrel dog frothing at the mouth. Such a rabid beast must be dealt with before he assaults everyone in his path!"

The other military men nodded in agreement.

"So if the persecution of Jews is your primary concern," Canaris continued, "the best way to stop that is to get rid of the one who is giving the orders. In fact, it is the only way, since—I am sure you have noticed—we no longer live in a democracy."

Dietrich nodded and sighed. "You make a very good case," he said to Canaris.

"There is one other thing you should think about," Hans broke in. "Since you are not yet forty years old, and are, for all practical purposes, unemployed, you would be subject to immediate call-up if a war begins. As a draftee, you would be required to sign a loyalty oath to the Führer. If you were to join the Abwehr, however, say, as some type of intelligence officer, you could sidestep both the oath and the prospect of being sent to the front. And I'm assuming you would like to avoid both of those prospects."

"The oath is more odious to me than the front line," Dietrich said, sighing again. "Hans, you are putting me in an impossible situation. First of all, what are the realistic chances that a putsch can be carried out?"

This time General Beck spoke up. "There is an upcoming meeting between the Führer and England's Prime Minister Chamberlain. It looks as if Hitler is going to demand that England look the other way when Germany invades the Sudetanland. Chamberlain will certainly refuse, but then Hitler will stubbornly go along with his plans. At that point he will be pushing things too far. Public opinion will turn against him. In the midst of the tumult, a group of officers close to the Führer will place him, Goebbels, Himmler, and the rest under arrest. If we time things correctly, it should work. Most of the generals feel as we do but are not willing to make the first move. Once that move is made, they will fall in line behind us."

"I'm impressed," Dietrich said while staring into the fireplace. "Of course I shall have to pray about making such a large step as joining the Abwehr in an official capacity, but until then I will help you in any way that I can. I agree that the persecutions, and everything else, must stop."

Hans looked at him and smiled. "I'm pleased, Dietrich."

Christine entered the room and took her brother's hands in her own. Her eyes were moist.

"Is there anything I can do right away?" Dietrich asked.

"Just one thing," Hans replied. "We need to get Gerhard and Sabine out of the country. Immediately."

On a cloud-filled October night, Dietrich pulled up at the Leibholz home in his parents' black sedan. Sabine had been watching for the headlights through the kitchen window, and when she saw them she gathered the children together. Gerhard grabbed his briefcase and the large suitcase that carried all the belongings the family would be taking with them. Then he led the way out through the side door of the house.

Dietrich met them with a grim smile and put the suitcase in the trunk of the car. The children had been told that they were merely going on a vacation, and for the first few miles they chattered about their individual vacation plans. Then Dietrich's seriousness began to dominate the mood within the car, and talk was kept to a minimum. Soon the children fell asleep.

Near morning, the car was met at the Swiss border by one of Dietrich's old friends from the ecumenical movement. This man vouched for the Leibholzes and gained their admittance into the country. But before the twin siblings parted ways, there were hugs, kisses, and weeping all around. Brother and sister assured each other that they would meet again soon, and Dietrich gave them his letter of introduction for the smoothing over of any bureaucratic difficulties.

Then Dietrich got into the car again and drove back to Berlin.

Two nights later, the greatest outbreak of violence against Jews up to that point in time occurred in Berlin and throughout the country. Roaming mobs smashed windows of Jewish-owned shops, and hundreds of synagogues were burned to the ground. Police were almost nonexistent, leaving individual German Jews defenseless against the rampaging and looting. The night would later become known as *Kristallnacht* ("the night of broken glass") in reference to all the glass that littered the sidewalks and streets. In many minds, this would be the true beginning of the Holocaust.

Kristallnacht justified Dietrich's action in getting Gerhard and Sabine out of the country, but it didn't make him feel any better about being separated from his twin. He had always felt a strange, almost mystical, bond to Sabine—they could always tell what the other was thinking

123

and feeling—and her flight was like an amputation to his psyche.

Yet, while Sabine's departure was devastating, there were several other challenges to his emotional and psychological well-being that winter.

First, the continued deterioration of the Confessing Church could not be ignored. An increasing number of ministers were willing to compromise on Nazi policies and pledge their loyalty to Hitler. Most of them did this because they had families to feed, but many also felt that Germany seemed to be on the rise again and they wanted to be a part of it. The allure of German nationalism was too strong for ministers to resist.

That wave of nationalism forced Dietrich to ponder his own eligibility for military service. Though Dietrich opposed war on just about every ground, he was personally not unwilling to fight if he were called up. After the war began, he even encouraged his former Finkenwalde students to be "soldiers among soldiers." What horrified him was the necessity of taking the military oath, which contained a promise to be personally loyal to Hitler himself. If he joined the Abwehr, he could at least temporarily avoid this dilemma because of the office's independence.

Still, that option had its drawbacks as Dietrich was extremely reluctant to get more deeply involved in the conspiracy. It still troubled his conscience as a Lutheran to go against the biblical injunction to submit to the ruling authorities. But the Bible also taught submission to authority in the Church, and he did not have any scruples about distinguishing between true and false authority there. As he prayed and thought about it more, he gradually came to believe that political revolution could also be justified without distorting Scripture. It would probably be impossible for Dietrich to join the Abwehr with a totally clear conscience, though.

A bigger problem for the moment, however, was the failure of General Beck to have correctly predicted the result of the Munich Conference between Hitler and Chamberlain. Hitler had turned on all of his charm at this meeting and convinced the British prime minister that Germany would be satisfied with annexing only the Sudetanland—and nothing more. The Sudetanland contained a primarily German population, anyway, Hitler argued. Chamberlain, in his now infamous act of appeasement, believed Hitler's promise and told him that England would not oppose any movement of German troops into the small strip of land that separated Germany from Czechoslovakia.

But Hitler used the Sudetanland as only the first step in his annexation of all of Czechoslovakia, making Chamberlain, who had gone back to London proclaiming "peace in our time," look like a fool. Even more disastrous, Hitler's "victory" at the Munich Conference had only strengthened his support among the German masses, which began to think that Providence was on the Führer's side. It seemed like he had superhuman wisdom. All of the popular support for a putsch that the Abwehr leadership had relied on before Munich dissolved into thin air. But instead of causing them to reconsider their goals, they instead reexamined their methods. Assassination began to be talked about as the only sure way of taking Hitler out.

Even though Dietrich was not aware of the assassination talk among the conspirators, he was discouraged by the general state of affairs and once again decided to leave the country for awhile. He desperately wanted to discuss the situation with Bishop Bell, whom he saw as a mentor. And if he went to London, he would also be able to visit Sabine and Gerhard, who had been forced out of Switzerland by the widening Gestapo net. So, after checking with Hans to see whether there was any Abwehr business he could do while in London, he left Germany in March of 1939.

Above all, he was looking for a chance to clear his mind. Lately, he had found it difficult even to pray.

fourteen

Engagement or Retreat

As a light snow fell outside the windows, Dietrich once again found himself within the pleasant confines of Bishop Bell's book-lined study, sipping tea and munching on scones. In such a haven, he felt that he could tell the bishop anything.

"So the military oath is your primary dilemma right now?" Bell asked.

"It is one of the biggest problems," Dietrich answered. "On Christian grounds, I find it difficult to do military service under the present conditions, and yet very few of my friends approve of this attitude. I have been thinking of going to the mission field, not as an escape, but because I wish to serve somewhere where service is really wanted and because I still see myself primarily as a pastor. But it is exceedingly difficult to find a mission board that will take someone like me."

"I'm sure that that is true," the bishop said. Then he

asked, "Is there anything for you to do in the ecumenical movement? It seems to me that they could always use someone of your talents and abilities."

"To be truthful," Dietrich answered, "I am thoroughly disenchanted with the movement—except for a few close friends who are still a part of it. I think the last straw was when they allowed Heckel and his entourage to attend the Winter Youth Conference. It was like a slap in the face of everyone who has been struggling."

"Then why not immerse yourself in the Confessing movement again? I know they have shut down the seminaries, but there has to be something for you there."

"I rather doubt it," Dietrich stated flatly, and the bishop reacted with an incredulous look.

"I'm sorry, Bishop," Dietrich continued, "but it is difficult to explain the sorry state of the church struggle these days. If the early leadership—people like Niemöller—weren't languishing in prison, perhaps things would be different, but. . . ." His voice drifted off.

"I'm not sure that I agree with your assessment of the two movements," the bishop responded. "I still work fairly closely with members of each. But I will not argue the point. What I really am curious about is the condition of your heart and mind. Where do you feel like God is leading you? What course of action would give you inward peace?"

"To be perfectly frank once again, dear Bishop, I'm not sure that I still have the luxury of knowing God's perfect will or of enjoying inner peace," Dietrich said, sinking deeper into his chair. "The situation really is impossible, and many responsible Christian men will find themselves in circumstances in which they will have to choose the lesser of two evils. No one will remain pure, unless he retires from an active life. Indeed, that is the real choice set before us—engagement or retreat. And I'm afraid that sin lies in both directions."

The bishop sat silently for a minute. Then he softly asked, "So what have you chosen, Dietrich, engagement or retreat?"

Dietrich rubbed at his eyes. Suddenly he felt very tired. "I have yet to choose," he admitted.

"Ah, I see." The bishop walked over to his desk, opened a drawer, and pulled out what looked to Dietrich like a datebook. He flipped through the pages. "Well, perhaps someone else can help you to make a decision better than I," he said, examining a particular page in the book. "Professor Niebuhr from America will be in London next week at a conference. Why don't you talk to him while he is here? I can set it up."

"Yes, maybe that is a good idea," Dietrich said, recalling how "old Reinie" had always been frank with him during his year in New York, eight years before. He thought that perhaps a little bit of good old American pragmatism might break the logjam in his mind.

He asked the bishop to make the appointment.

"Why don't you come to New York?" Niebuhr asked Dietrich as they walked along the fence line of the country estate where the American theologian was staying.

Dietrich shook his head slowly. "But how could I justify such a trip at this time?"

"How can you justify staying?" Niebuhr retorted. "The Confessing Church is in ruins. Hitler is poised to take over Eastern Europe. You don't have a church, job, or even a country anymore. In the States, you could try to convince some of our lunkhead diplomats that the situation is severe. It's clear that most of them think that old Adolf only wants *Eastern* Europe, and they don't particularly care about Eastern Europe. They forget that Versailles is still a burr in the Führer's side and that France is probably next on his shopping list. To be entirely honest, I'm afraid that England isn't that safe, either."

"Yes, I tend to agree with you," Dietrich said.

"So of course the only option for someone like you is to do some good on the other side of the Atlantic, where it *is* relatively safe. I can even set up a class or two for you to teach at Union, just to keep you plenty busy."

"I–I–I don't know," Dietrich stammered.

"Really now, Dietrich," Niebuhr exclaimed. "If you don't come, you are sure to get stuck in Berlin with a uniform on your back and a gun in your hands. That would be quite a sight, considering the pacifist principles you attempt to espouse. Can you really see yourself in such a getup?"

"It is difficult, "Dietrich agreed, "but there might be other options." He was thinking about Hans and the Abwehr.

"Perhaps so," Niebuhr said as he stopped to lean against the fence and look out over the fields that were scattered with spring flowers. "But you have to decide what your *best* option is. Once you have figured that out, then you only have to choose. It is really quite simple."

Dietrich smiled in response. "You were always good at simplification, Herr Professor," he said.

"And you were always good at making things too complicated," Niebuhr shot back, laughing and slapping Dietrich on the back. "I remember that during your trip to

Union you used to spend a whole week of class time differentiating between Augustine's and Luther's definitions of a *just war*. The students complained to me that your head was so full of abstract questions and reservations that living in the real world was difficult for you. And I must admit that I tended to agree with them. Sometimes in the real world you can't find the ideal situation. You have to just accept the next-best situation and not beat yourself up over it."

Dietrich had a pained look on his face. "But is that a *Christian* view of things?"

Niebuhr chuckled. "I don't know, but that's the world of the Bible. People did things without thinking too much." Then he paused. "Especially when they were hungry." The tone of his voice had changed. "So what do you say we go back to the house and find some corned beef, or whatever else these Brits keep in their pantries."

Chuckling also, Dietrich agreed. For the first time in several weeks, he actually had an appetite

Dietrich's few remaining weeks in London were spent with Sabine and Gerhard. He went to great lengths to help Gerhard make some connections and to reestablish a law practice. In the evenings, he would stay up past midnight with Sabine, reminiscing about childhood days.

But in the back of his mind, he was constantly ruminating about the decision before him—whether to go back to Germany and throw himself fully into the resistance (which he had come to recognize as his only real option in Germany) or to go to America and do all the good that he could from there. Niebuhr's advice about the importance of taking action was all well and good, but it was not Dietrich's way to act first and think later. All he could do was remain true to who he was.

In the end, neither direction seemed particularly compelling or righteous. Consequently, he decided to do what would probably enable him to evade the tremendous threat to his identity that the conspiracy represented. The following month, he boarded a boat for New York City.

He was not entirely sure why he was going.

New York was a bustle of activity in the summer of 1939. It was the year of the World's Fair and the city was like a teeming global village. Africans in flowing, multicolored robes could be seen walking down the street shoulder to shoulder with ruddy-cheeked Australians. Brazilians and Swedes sat in adjoining booths at corner delicatessens. And everybody seemed happy to be there. Everybody, that is, except Dietrich, who wasn't sure how he felt.

He spent most of his time in his well-furnished apartment on the Union campus, working on lectures for a class Niebuhr had set up for him to teach. Invitations to parties and get-togethers were in his mailbox every day, but he declined most of them, responding with short and polite notes. He excused himself with declarations about how busy he was, but in truth he was only revising lectures that he had already given in Berlin. He spent his time mainly lying on his bed, thinking and praying about the same things over and over again.

In the first week, he met with several U.S. diplomats, whom he found strangely unwilling to believe his carefully worded claims about the burgeoning resistance movement in Germany. Like Winston Churchill, who had replaced Chamberlain as British prime minister, they simplified things by preferring to see Germans as unanimously supportive of Hitler and his policies. No matter how much Dietrich explained the intricacy of the situation, all parties preferred to believe their own less complex version of events, as if Dietrich were surely mistaken about what he had observed firsthand. After awhile, he found it less distressing to keep to himself and not talk about Germany at all.

He would have successfully isolated himself were it not for Niebuhr, who came around regularly and forced him to leave his apartment. One evening, out of a sense of obligation, Dietrich went to a faculty member's home for dinner. There, he was introduced to some of the most prominent pastors in the city. These men were much more receptive to Dietrich's view of the situation in Germany than the U.S. government had been. In fact, they were so disturbed that they decided to hold an impromptu prayer meeting after dinner. Although Dietrich was deeply moved by their heartfelt prayers for "our German brethren," the prayers also served to heighten Dietrich's homesickness and to bother his injured sense of duty.[1]

The next day, he wandered around the city alone, taking in the sights and silently praying about his future. He had not received any news from home, and he was starving for information. He needed to feel connected. The newspapers only reported increasing threats from Goebbels and other Nazi leaders against Poland. This was the big picture. War was inevitable. But Dietrich yearned to be involved in what was going on behind the scenes. By coming to America he had, in effect, absolved himself from any responsibility for Germany's path and future. Yet he still felt that he had a duty under God to be responsible—to experience Germany's fate as a German, whether it threatened the purity of his conscience or not. In his heart, he knew that coming to America had not been the path of true faith. He had chosen safety rather than risk.

That evening, Dietrich wrote in his diary: "We can, in fact, justify anything; but in the last resort we are acting from a plane that is hidden from us; and we can only ask God to judge and forgive us."[2]

Then, taking another sheet of paper, he began a letter to Niebuhr.

I have made a terrible mistake in coming to America. I must live through this difficult period of our national history with the Christian people of Germany. I will have no right to participate in the reconstruction of Christian life in Germany after the war if I do not share the trials of this time with my people. . . . Christians in Germany will face the terrible alternative of either willing the defeat of their nation in order that Christian civilization may survive, or willing the victory of their nation and thereby destroying our civilization. I know which of these alternatives I must choose; but I cannot make the choice in security![3]

fifteen

Never Safe Again

Dietrich's plane landed in Berlin on July 27, 1939. Though he would leave his home country again on several occasions, gone was the feeling that he was evading his responsibility. He was back for the duration this time, however long that might be.

In America, Dietrich had felt safe and righteous. The feeling of safety was understandable for obvious reasons, but the feeling of righteousness was more complicated. Americans had seen him as someone who had already suffered. They had read about the church struggle and about the courageous decisions that had been made by the Confessing movement. Dietrich had been one of those few who had already stood up to Hitler, or at least to Hitler's emissaries. And he was sensitive enough to know that the Americans admired him for this.

But he felt righteous because he had never compromised himself. He had stuck to his pacifist principles until it became clear that they were not going to change the course of events. Then he left. It was logical for him to leave the country once he could not do anything else to save it, he had reasoned. To have stayed would have been to enter into the heart of darkness along with his country. And despite all of his experiences, that was something he could hardly bear to think about. To be a man of peace during times of peace was relatively easy. To be a man of peace during a general European war was probably impossible— unless one chose to live in a cave somewhere.

No, war forced men to make choices between two (or three or four) evils; it forced even the pious to become "worldly" in order to live wholly as men. Dietrich knew this and still chose to go back. He would never be entirely safe again. Neither would he be entirely righteous. All he could do was trust that God would forgive him.

Yet at first there was not a lot for him to do. After the Munich Conference, plans for a putsch were temporarily shelved. Dietrich met with Hans and offered to be of help, but he was not ready to formally join the Abwehr yet. He simply told Hans that he wanted to be "useful," and Hans told him to keep in touch.

On September 1, 1939, Germany invaded Poland and World War II began. Dietrich was now vulnerable to military call-up, but until the call came he involved himself in Confessing Church activities and wrote letters to former students who were in the army. He was especially pained when Theodor Maas, one of the quieter students at Finkenwalde, was killed in action in Poland.

As far as the Confessing Church, Dietrich was still pressing its leadership to take a stronger stand on controversial issues. This time he wanted the Church to speak out against the war itself. What did it have to lose, he reasoned. Yet many of the church leaders were frightened of the consequences. No patriotic German was speaking out against what had turned out to be a very successful series of military actions. The leadership of the Church wanted to stick entirely to theological issues, and thus in Dietrich's eyes they were becoming increasingly irrelevant. At one time he had been adamant about the need for a theological resistance to the Reich Church, but events had gone beyond that now. It was too late for the Church to confine itself to such narrow concerns.

Because of Dietrich's outspoken views since his return to Berlin, the Gestapo was keeping its eye on him. He was already on public record as a dissenter to the regime, and anything he did now or said would be seen in the worst possible light. This became apparent the next summer when he organized a Bible conference in which members of the Confessing movement were the most prominent invitees. The Gestapo saw this conference as a possible cover for conspiratorial activities and shut it down. Dietrich protested, even using his family name to pull rank, but it got him nowhere. He was soon thereafter forbidden to speak in public and was even "requested" to report regularly to the police.

In the autumn of 1940, Dietrich was being drawn inexorably into the protective arms of the Abwehr. Joining the counterintelligence would protect him from military call-up and prevent him from having to take the loyalty oath. It would also allow him to shape the new constitution of his country after a successful takeover. On the other hand, it would force him to be a double agent, someone who would constantly be pretending to be someone that he was not. No longer would he be able to retreat into the safe haven of a pastorate. His life would be at constant risk until the Nazis were dislodged from power. The truth was, he would have to practice deception in order to stay alive.

Dietrich had already got a taste for this sort of life the previous June while attending a pastor's conference in the city of Memel. He and his friend Eberhard Bethge were relaxing on the terrace of a café when the news was announced that Paris had fallen. The people immediately stood to their feet and cheered, thrusting their arms out in the Nazi salute. Bethge was surprised to see Dietrich also spring to his feet and shout "Heil Hitler!" When Bethge remained sitting, Dietrich bent down and whispered in his ear, "Stand up, you fool. This is not worth getting noticed for." Bethge, who was astonished at the way his friend could so cunningly play the role of the loyal Nazi, quickly got up from his seat.

It was thus not surprising that Dietrich offered himself in November to the Abwehr as a full-fledged agent. His reasoning was that only in the Abwehr would he be able to "work for the defeat of his country" in a way that made the most effective use of his talents and resources. He also realized, after the fall of Paris, that Hitler was firmly entrenched in power, with the support of the masses behind him. He would not be taken out of the way as easily as had been hoped. It would take persistent effort, possibly over the course of years, to undermine the regime. Hence, offering his services to the Abwehr seemed like the only responsible path, and Hans quickly assigned Dietrich to the organization's Munich office.

Since there was not much for him to do right away, that winter Dietrich took the opportunity of staying with monks at a Benedictine Abbey near Munich in order to work, ironically, on a book about ethics. It was somewhat strange for him to be in the peaceful atmosphere of the monastery while the war was progressing on two fronts, but to Dietrich it seemed like a special gift of grace. Following the daily schedule of the monastery helped him to settle his thoughts and truly meditate on Scripture. In a November letter to Bethge, Dietrich wrote about the pleasures of staying at the monastery:

> *I'm still a guest [here]. The ordered life suits me
> very well, and I'm surprised at the similarity
> to much of what we did of our own accord at
> [Finkenwalde]. . . . The natural hospitality, which
> is evidently something specifically Benedictine, the
> really Christian respect for strangers for Christ's
> sake, almost makes one ashamed. You should come
> here some time! It's a real experience. . . .*[1]

Yet his thoughts often returned to Sabine, to the failed church struggle, and to the state of Protestantism in general. It seemed that the whole world was falling apart in an orgy of suffering and pain while the Church was strangely impotent, even unconcerned, to do anything to stem the tide. Dietrich admired the constancy of the Catholicism that he experienced at the monastery, and that he had seen in Rome, but he still thought that the Protestant heritage, if regained, was best equipped to deal with the real spiritual problems of the modern world. For Dietrich, Protestantism ideally meant that one could not hide behind "religion" and culture. One was forced to confront the naked facts of one's existence and then respond to those facts with faith, even if it seemed impossible. Again, the only path of discipleship was the path that led through the cross.

Finally, in February, Hans called upon Dietrich to go to Switzerland and make contacts with those who might be willing to receive expatriate Jews into the country. Dietrich's job was to prepare the way for what would later be called "Operation 7," an operation that saw dozens of Jews successfully escape Germany under the auspices of the Abwehr. The Abwehr justified this to the Nazi hierarchy by calling it a foreign relations ploy. The Jews would supposedly be instructed to say good things about the Nazi regime.

The Gestapo quickly became suspicious, though, making the operation much riskier. Indeed, a couple of years later, the Gestapo's investigation into the Abwehr's use of funds during Operation 7 led to the discovery of incriminating documents that caused the arrest of Dietrich and the Abwehr leadership. Before this happened, though, the Abwehr was able to accomplish a great deal.

The year 1941 saw a dramatic escalation of events in the war and within Germany itself. In April, German troops invaded Yugoslavia and Greece. On May 23, most of the remaining leadership of the Confessing Church was arrested. On June 22, German troops invaded the Soviet Union. On September 19, a decree was issued that required all German Jews to wear a yellow star stitched to their clothing. In October, the first gas chambers were installed in Auschwitz, Poland. On December 7, Japan attacked Pearl Harbor, Hawaii, bringing the United States fully into the war. And in January of 1942, the Nazi leadership agreed to implement a "Final Solution" policy that called for the extermination of all Jews in Germany and occupied territories.

Throughout 1941, most of Dietrich's actions as a double

agent for the Abwehr happened under a thick cloak of secrecy. He traveled back and forth between Munich and Switzerland, meeting with contacts that had access to foreign leaders. The constant goal was to convince the Americans and the British that there was a well-organized, yet hidden, resistance within the Nazi hierarchy itself. But the Allies would not be convinced until they saw some tangible results from the supposed resistance, thus catching the conspirators in a vicious circle: They needed outside support for their plans to succeed, yet the outside help would not be forthcoming until they succeeded.

Dietrich had a key role in this extremely difficult task of bringing foreign support to the cause. In May of 1942, he traveled to Sigtuna, Sweden, to talk to Bishop Bell on behalf of the resistance. Little did they realize that this would be the last time they would see each other. Dietrich urged Bell to try to convince Prime Minister Churchill that there was a valid conspiracy working to topple Hitler, and that people were in place to take over and restore a democratic government that would be acceptable to the Allies. All they needed was a lull in the war to put their plan in motion.

Even though Bell promised to do his best, he was unsuccessful. Churchill was not willing to shape his war effort to meet the needs of a "shadow" conspiracy. He was determined to conquer Germany itself, whether Hitler was there or not.

Now that Dietrich was "active," in the sense that Niebuhr had urged, he became even more aware of the impotence of the churches. Except for the prayers of a small number, nothing significant was happening among the Christians of

Germany to stem the tide of lawlessness in their midst. To Dietrich, this refusal to get involved was not because of piety but rather a lack of moral courage. Dwelling as he was in the land of Luther, this cowardice was astounding to him. Yet, how many times had he seen this willingness to withdraw in the "religious" side of himself?

He repeatedly reflected on how easy it was to exit the discomforts of this world for the comforts of a more spiritual one, as in the following excerpt from a letter to Bethge:

> *I detect that a rebellion against all things "religious" is growing in me. Often it amounts to an instinctive horror—which is certainly not good. I'm not religious by nature. But I have to think continually of God and Christ; authenticity, life, freedom, and mercy mean a great deal to me. It is just their religious manifestations which are so unattractive. Do you understand?[2]*

That Nazism could arise in one of the most Christian nations in Europe was an abiding concern of Dietrich's. It fed his increasing criticism of religion as a social construction that was opposed to faith itself. Later, this line of thinking would lead him to look for what he would shockingly call "a religionless Christianity." But most of his thoughts on this matter would not be more fully developed until he had the leisure to sit down and work them out.

Unfortunately, this leisure would not be his until he was a prisoner of the regime.

sixteen

Love and Assassination

In the spring of 1942 a joyful complication by the name of Maria von Wedemeyer entered Dietrich's life. She was the granddaughter of Ruth von Kleist-Retzow, one of the early benefactors of Finkenwalde seminary, and she had first met Dietrich when she was twelve years old. Dietrich, of course, did not notice her then, since she was a shy, barely adolescent girl. He had merely been asked to prepare her and her older sister for confirmation, and this employment was a small part of his life at the time. But six years later, Maria had grown into a beautiful young woman, who would not be so easily shuffled to the corners of his consciousness.

Initially, tragedy brought them together again. Maria's father (and Ruth's son-in-law) was killed on the eastern front. Dietrich heard about it because he had always tried to stay in touch with Maria's grandmother. Ruth von Kleist-Retzow, besides having been one of the most constant supporters of the Confessing Church, also possessed a nimble theological mind. Dietrich liked to discuss the writings of Barth and other prominent theologians with her whenever he had the chance. Over time, they had grown to be close friends.

Thus, when Dietrich received a telegram from her informing him of Count von Wedemeyer's death, he dropped everything and rushed to the family house in Klein-Kossin to lend emotional support.

Soon after he arrived, though, he was smitten by the presence of his former catechism student. He could not believe at first that she was the same girl. She was no longer shy, and she met his gaze with eyes that were deep and lustrous, yet soft and unassuming. Her evident maturity, as shown in the way she helped her mother to greet the visitors, belied her eighteen years.

Dietrich did not reveal his immediate feelings at this time since it would not have been appropriate, but he did strike up a private conversation with Maria at the first opportunity. It occurred late in the afternoon when most of the visitors had left to go to their own homes for dinner. Somehow the two of them started talking about mathematics, and though neither of them knew much about the subject, they ended up talking for several hours. For all that Dietrich cared, they could have been talking about spiders. The conversation would not have been any less pleasant.

Despite the instant rapport between them, Dietrich and Maria did not see each other again until the fall when Maria came to Berlin to take care of her grandmother. They had both been in each other's thoughts almost constantly, so Dietrich was overjoyed when Maria wrote him, telling him of her presence in Berlin. He hastily arranged his schedule so that he could see her.

With some distance between her and the rest of her family, Maria was much more outgoing and boisterous than she had been before in Dietrich's presence. As a country girl, she was eager to see the sights of Berlin, and Dietrich was eager to act as her tour guide. Berlin, even with swastika flags draped everywhere, was still the city in all the world that was closest to his heart, and he joyously took Maria through the vast museums, sprawling city gardens, and architectural wonders that made this one of the cultural centers of Europe. They also visited shops where Maria bought souvenirs for herself and her siblings. Dietrich felt as if he could walk forever and not get tired, but when Maria took off her heels to carry them, they finally did stop at a sidewalk café.

As they sat at a small table, Dietrich was suddenly struck dumb. He could not believe what was happening. The outside world was in chaos, Germany was inflamed with military fervor, Dietrich himself was involved in schemes to undermine the Third Reich—and all he could think of was his growing love for a young woman he barely knew. It was so incredible, Dietrich even questioned whether it could truly be God's will.

"What are you thinking about, Dietrich?" Maria asked, snatching him out of his reverie. Her voice was low but melodious.

"Oh, nothing really," he responded.

"Do you want to go somewhere?"

"Oh no, not at all."

He realized that he had no idea how to express what he was feeling, especially since the Abwehr had trained him to be less expressive about what he was thinking, and not more. And the age difference only made him less at ease.

145

Finally he decided to break the silence by asking about Maria's family.

"Oh, Mother is doing well," Maria said. "She doesn't like for me to be out of her sight, but I slip away whenever I can."

Dietrich smiled.

"It's strange," she continued. "I feel all grown up, but nobody except you really treats me like an adult yet. I am constantly being watched over."

This was something that Dietrich had been worried about—that Maria's family would take exception to their age difference and disallow a relationship. He said to her, "You seem very mature to me. I'm sure that everyone else will soon recognize that. It's only a matter of time and patience."

"I suppose so," Maria answered, looking down the street at the row of shops. "But I really do need to tell you something, Dietrich."

"Yes?"

"I have to tell you that Mother really doesn't approve of our seeing one another."

This is it, Dietrich thought. His fears had been realized. "Is it because of the age difference?" he asked, already supposing that he knew the answer.

"Well, that's part of it," she said, taking another sip of her coffee. "But what really concerns her is that you are not a military man. All of the women in our family have married officers, and Mother can't understand why a man of your age has not made a career in some *manly* profession."

Dietrich was both horrified and ready to howl with laughter. He could not tell from Maria's expression whether she was teasing him or being absolutely serious.

146

"Hmm," was all he could say. But then he remembered that she had mentioned something about marriage.

"Not that it matters to me," Maria continued. "Both Grandmother and I know what kind of man you are. And even if my mother does not approve," she said, pausing, "I do."

Dietrich smiled. "I can't tell you how glad I am to hear that," he said.

In the spring of 1942, Operation 7 became a reality. After months of intricate planning, the Abwehr was successful in getting a small group of Jews into Switzerland and out of the reach of the Gestapo. They were intent on this operation because of the increasing roundups of Jews from all over Germany, with most ending up in death camps. Dietrich's activities in this operation—securing living arrangements in Switzerland for the group and then taking part in the transport—proved his absolute commitment to the political resistance of the Abwehr. Hans now felt that he could trust him with anything.

It was a two-way street, though, as Dietrich used Hans to get military deferments for former pastors of the Confessing movement who were vulnerable to military call-up. Many were assigned to far-flung Abwehr offices and given honorary titles such as "Intelligence Officer," thus enabling them to avoid the draft. Even though he drew suspicion from the Gestapo for doing this, Hans was more than happy to relieve Dietrich of the agony of seeing more of his former students and colleagues killed in Hitler's war.

Throughout late spring and summer, Dietrich tried to finish and revise his book on ethics, but Hans called upon him much more frequently than before, causing him to put off his theological work indefinitely. He was willing to do anything he could to help, though, and in May when Hans asked him to go to Norway, Dietrich was especially eager to go.

Norway had fallen to Germany early in the war, and the Reich Church had tried to enforce its discipline upon the national Protestant church there, which was also Lutheran. Contrary to the sequence of events in Germany, though, the Lutheran pastors in Norway decided in April of 1942 to go on strike rather than compromise their theological beliefs. This action brought about the arrest of the senior bishop of the Lutheran Church in Norway, a man by the name of Berggrav.

Hans sent Dietrich, along with another resister named von Moltke, to observe the events firsthand. Officially, they were going there under the auspices of the Abwehr to look for ways to put down the resistance, but their intentions were to do the exact opposite.

Dietrich was fascinated by the situation in Norway because the collective action of the pastors there was exactly the kind of dramatic response he had pushed for in the German churches years earlier. Now it was Norway, to the shame of the German churches, which was providing the model for the effective resistance of a Lutheran church to state domination. And to Dietrich's and von Moltke's delight, they found the resistance in Norway to be unbending in its resolve. It was clear that Hitler would never be able to put them entirely under his boot.

In July, Dietrich traveled with Hans to Italy in an attempt to forge a relationship with the resistance there, but they found that the opponents of Fascism in Italy had been weakened by recent German victories. Morale was low. Yet

Dietrich and Hans were successful in strengthening ties between the German resistance and the Vatican, where an Abwehr man, Josef Muller, was permanently assigned.

Throughout the fall and winter, while Dietrich was helping Hans to unify the various pockets of resistance within Germany and plan for the subsequent assassination attempts, his relationship with Maria was also escalating. Though they were rarely able to see one another, they kept in touch through postcards and occasional phone calls. Still, this limited contact was enough to cement their intentions toward one another, and at Christmas they approached Maria's mother to express their desire to be engaged.

"No, certainly not! Maria is much too young," Frau von Wedemeyer responded initially. But Dietrich would not be deterred. He knew that he needed Maria at this time in his life, and he was convinced that it was God's will for them to be together. Maria felt the same way but was less willing to defy her mother.

Nevertheless, through a combination of charm and determination, Dietrich finally gained Frau von Wedemeyer's blessing. She asked only that they keep the engagement a secret for the time being, or at least until Maria had reached her twentieth birthday. The couple agreed, and as it turned out, their engagement was not made public until after Dietrich had been taken to Tegel prison.

Dietrich would later wonder whether he had been selfish in forcing the issue with Maria's mother. He questioned whether, under the circumstances, he should have been so eager to lock Maria into a commitment that could possibly conflict with his other serious commitment. But he also had been fully confident that winter about the chances for the resistance to overthrow the Nazi regime. He clearly envisioned Maria and himself starting their life and family together in a post-Hitler Germany. The engagement had merely been an expression of that optimism and faith. If such a step had also been unnecessarily risky and a tad foolhardy, well, that could only be blamed on the nature of love.

As winter progressed, though, the news from the Russian front was not good for the conspirators. German troops were getting bogged down deep in Russian territory, and it seemed for the first time that military defeat on a wide scale was possible. It was imperative that Hitler be taken out of the way before Germany went down to defeat, since the Allies would not be merciful toward a defeated Germany that was still under his leadership. The conspirators were desperate to get another government in place so that they might surrender under terms that would be beneficial to the future of Germany. They knew that their country would have to be punished, but they did not want it to be destroyed.

Once the various centers of the resistance were coordinated, plans for the assassination of the Führer went into high gear. The first attempt would be made on the eastern front in March of 1943. The conspirators saw their opportunity when Hitler went to Smolensk to receive progress reports from his generals and to observe the morale of the troops. While he was there, an English-made bomb was placed on his return plane by an agent of the Abwehr. It was set to detonate while the plane was in the air. The planning had been rushed, but it had also been meticulous. Thus, there was surprise throughout the resistance when it was reported that Hitler had safely landed in Germany again. For some unknown reason, the bomb had failed to detonate.

Luckily, it had also been undetected.

The second attempt was made two weeks later. Hitler was scheduled to tour an armory where trophies of war were being displayed. A decorated war hero, Major von Gersdorff, volunteered to carry out the suicide mission. He was placed by the Abwehr as one of Hitler's tour guides and agreed to carry two explosive devices in his pockets. When Hitler stood next to him, he would detonate both of these and kill everyone within a ten-foot radius.

On the evening of the assassination attempt, both Dietrich and Hans were at Dietrich's sister Ursula's home. They, along with other family members, were practicing a selection of musical pieces for Karl Bonhoeffer's seventy-fifth birthday party the next day. Dietrich played the piano in his usual enthusiastic style, and Hans sang. No one in the family had the slightest hint that both of them were waiting for the telephone to ring, telling them of the success of the mission. Hans's car even sat in the driveway with its motor running, so that he could leave immediately to help with the reconstruction of the government.

But the telephone call never came. For some reason, Hitler had decided to cut his trip to the armory short. He never got anywhere near von Gersdorff.

Incredibly, the Führer had now survived two well-planned, and seemingly foolproof, attempts on his life. Could it be that he truly was under divine protection?

A week later, before any other attempts could be made, the Gestapo was deep enough into its investigation of Operation 7 to issue warrants for the arrest of Dietrich and Hans. Both were taken into custody on the same day.

151

seventeen

Tegel Prison

The days in Tegel prison fell into a routine, especially after Dietrich was able to receive books from the outside world. He would wake up at 6 A.M. and splash his face from a bowl of lukewarm water. Then he would read portions of whatever volumes had been sent in his latest parcel. Sometimes there were works of theology, sometimes philosophy or history, but more and more Dietrich was drawn to novels and poetry, especially the works of nineteenth-century German writers.

The romantic style of this literature reminded him of his youthful idealism for his homeland. At one time, he had believed Germany to be the purest and noblest nation in the world. But then, when similar ideas allowed the Nazis to rise to power, he recognized that his notion was part of a larger, and very dangerous, national myth. For the past ten years, his most enduring feeling about his country was that of shame and disappointment. He was not angry with his countrymen, or at least he wasn't anymore. Now he only pitied them, praying for them constantly.

After reading for a couple of hours, Dietrich would try to write. He wrote letters to family members or friends, and he took notes for the large book on ethics that he had begun before his arrest. But in keeping with his reading, he was also trying to write a novel. The story was about a family not unlike his own, an aristocratic clan that tried to hold to its values in the midst of social turmoil. Dietrich had never tried to compose a narrative before, yet the writing filled him with a deep sense of joy and satisfaction. And though he suspected the novel would never be published, or even be read by anyone other than himself, he felt compelled to keep at it. Something about putting his own experiences into a made-up story helped keep his mind on an even keel.

After a lunch of dark bread and watered-down coffee, Dietrich was usually taken into the prison yard so that he could walk. During these exercise periods, Dietrich took the opportunity to talk with Corporal Linke about his mail. Linke would let him know if his letters had made it past the censor, and also if any packages had reached the prison that morning. The prison officials usually only allowed each prisoner one package per week, so Dietrich did not always ask Linke if a parcel had arrived. He knew that he was likely to be disappointed.

Sometimes Dietrich was surprised by unexpected visitors during his exercise time—either his parents, one of his sisters, or, on the most blessed occasions, Maria.

The engaged couple was never allowed to meet entirely in private, nor was Dietrich ever told beforehand that Maria was there. This arrangement was just another of the Nazis' subtle but cruel methods of emotional torture. Naturally,

Dietrich would have much rather had a few days to prepare for Maria's visits. Then he could have experienced the intense joy and pain of looking forward to seeing her, counting down the days and hours and minutes until he was led into her presence. It would have made time seem more valuable and real to him.

Instead, he would be led from the yard in a routine manner and made to believe that he was going to be interrogated. Then he would enter a room, and Maria would be sitting there, radiant and flushed in all her youthful beauty. Of course, she would also be accompanied by a Gestapo agent, who would sit surreptitiously in a corner to record anything in their conversation that might be useful to the ongoing investigation. And there was always the guard who remained inside the door.

But at least she was actually there—not as a vision of Dietrich's fevered imagination, but undeniably in the flesh.

The first time this occurred, the effect of unexpectedly seeing Maria nearly buckled him at the knees. She was wearing a plain blue summer dress, and her face and arms were slightly sunburned. He almost fell toward her, and involuntary tears filled her eyes. The Gestapo agent in the corner said, "You have fifteen minutes," and they spent the first five simply gazing into each other's faces. Then words tumbled out in a torrent, primarily from Dietrich, who had already lost some of his aristocratic reserve in prison. He was not ashamed at all to profess his love for her in the most effusive terms. Then he would ask about her family and his family and press her for every detail of everybody's lives.

Maria was primarily concerned about Dietrich's health. In his first months at Tegel, he had lost twenty pounds, which had caused his face to lose its former fullness. It was more drawn, making him look older and tired, and his eyes seemed to have sunk deeper into their sockets. Little in Maria's life experience had prepared her for this type of situation, and she often wondered whether she could actually endure it.

But Dietrich ended their first meeting with stern admonitions for her to keep the faith. As he did this, he would take on a fatherly tone with her.

> *You must remember to read and memorize Scripture. It will maintain your strength better than anything else. . . .*
>
> *Be sure to pray for all of us in here. Some of these men are miserable to the point of death. . . .*
>
> *Tell my parents that I am doing very well and getting a lot of study and work done. . . .*
>
> *Now you must remember to treat your mother well and to not pull away from her, no matter how grumpy she gets. . . .*

Maria listened meekly to these instructions and diligently obeyed them, but she often wondered how things would have been different if Dietrich were closer to her own age. Would they be on a more equal plane, or would he still talk to her like that because he was a man? She didn't know. But she still loved and admired him and did not want to disappoint him in any way while he was in prison.

A little while after her first visit, Maria received a letter from Dietrich that was meant to strengthen her in the belief that their relationship was still ordained by God. He seemed to have an inkling of her doubts as he wrote the following:

You cannot imagine what it means in my present situation to have you. I am certain of God's special guidance here. The way in which we found each other and the time, so shortly before my imprisonment, are a clear sign of this. . . . Every day I am overcome anew at how undeservedly I received this happiness, and each day I am deeply moved at what a hard school God has led you through during the last year. And now it appears to be His will that I have to bring you sorrow and suffering. . .so that our love for each other may achieve the right foundation and the right endurance. When I also think about the situation of the world, the complete darkness over our personal fate and my present imprisonment, then I believe that our union can only be a sign of God's grace and kindness, which calls us to faith. We would be blind if we did not see it. Jeremiah says at the moment of his people's great need "still one shall buy houses and acres in this land" as a sign of trust in the future. This is where faith belongs. May God give it to us daily. And I do not mean the faith which flees the world, but the one that endures the world and which loves and remains true to the world in spite of all the suffering which it contains for us. Our marriage shall be a yes to God's earth; it shall strengthen our courage to accomplish something on the earth. I fear that Christians who stand with only one leg upon earth also stand with only one leg in heaven.[1]

During Dietrich's first few months at Tegel, he had hopes

that his imprisonment would only be temporary. If he had suspected its permanence, it is doubtful that he would have filled Maria with false hopes and encouraged her to remain engaged to him. But he knew that Hans had covered all of their tracks very well, and that the Gestapo had little or no evidence to keep the conspirators in prison for long. The only factor that could extend their stay—and this was a factor that could not be underestimated—was the paranoia of the Nazi hierarchy. This consideration made everything unpredictable.

As time went on, Dietrich still tried to keep a hopeful tone in his letters to Maria, but it became increasingly difficult. His ability to see God's hand in their separation wavered yet was not entirely lost. As a man who was eager to get married, he saw it all as a tremendous test of his faith. In a letter to Maria the following fall, he wrote:

> *Slowly it gets to be a waiting whose outward sense I cannot comprehend; the inward reason must be found daily. Both of us have lost infinitely much during the past months; time today is a costly commodity, for who knows how much more time is given to us. And yet I do not dare to think that it was, or is, lost time. . . . We have grown together in a different way than we have thought and wished, but these are unusual times and will remain so awhile longer, and everything depends on our being one in the essential things and on our remaining with each other. Your life would have been quite different, easier, clearer, simpler had not our paths crossed a year ago. But there are only short moments when this thought bothers me. . . .[2]*

When Maria received this letter, she immediately sat down and wrote back to him in words that he must have longed to hear.

> *Dietrich, there are bound to be times when*
> *we're angry or depressed or despairing, but they*
> *mustn't outweigh the two of us and our together-*
> *ness. I've always found it incomprehensible that*
> *they haven't done so—no thanks to me. But now*
> *I, too, know that they can never become too*
> *much for us. Thank you for being the way*
> *you are, for all you're enduring and doing*
> *for my sake.*[3]

A much more unpleasant interruption to Dietrich's daily routine was his occasional visit to the prison courtroom. He was summoned there once or twice a week by a Nazi special investigator named Sonderegger who was primarily interested in Dietrich's activities as a member of the Abwehr.

The avoidance of regular military service was something that especially interested Sonderegger, and he relentlessly grilled Dietrich about his motives for avoiding the draft.

The special investigator and his assistants had not been able to find many records of Dietrich's activities during the past several years. And since the Abwehr was very good at hiding its documents, it looked as if he had done little, an impression that Dietrich was eager to maintain. The less the Nazis knew, the better.

"Do you think it is very patriotic to sit around doing practically nothing while Germany's sons are dying on the battlefield?" Sonderegger asked at one point.

"I did not look at it as doing nothing," Dietrich responded. "I was on call at all times to carry out whatever the Abwehr required."

"It doesn't look like they called on you to do very much."

"Not as much as I would have liked," Dietrich slyly answered.

During the afternoon Dietrich did more walking in his cell, and his days usually ended with a supper of watery soup, maybe an inspection of his cell, and more study or letter writing until it was time for "lights out" at eight.

One evening he wrote a letter to Hans, who was suffering from phlebitis in a prison at Potsdam.

My dear Hans, you must know that there is not even an atom of reproach or bitterness in me about what has befallen the two of us. Such things come from God and from Him alone, and I know that I am one with you and Christine in believing that before Him there can only be subjection, perseverance, patience—and gratitude. I now want you to know that since January I have been engaged to Maria von Wedemeyer. Because of the deaths of her father and brother, it was not to be mentioned until the summer, and I was only to tell my parents. It's a severe trial for Maria, but her mother writes that she is brave, cheerful, and confident, so that is a very great encouragement to me. I'm reading, learning, and working a great deal and have a quiet time in the morning and evening to think of all the many people, at home and in the field, whom one would and could commend each day to God.

I need not say that now you and Christine have a special place among them. God bless you. I think of you faithfully each day. Your Dietrich.[4]

What he really wanted to tell Hans was that he had not betrayed the resistance. But of course he could not do that with the Nazi censor reading his every word. It would have made his claim into a lie.

eighteen

The Sick Ward

Dietrich found himself waking up most mornings with a prayer on his lips. He was praying more than ever before, yet he felt no special sense of God's presence in the prison. He only felt his responsibility to be a man of God and, if necessary, to suffer where God had placed him. He was starting to think that true faith did not involve feelings at all—that it was instead the God-given ability to respond in love to the world as it was. Faith was no escape hatch from the power of evil men; true faith often placed one directly in the grip of evil. Hadn't Jesus Himself provided a demonstration of this truth?

One morning, Dietrich walked by himself in the prison yard, mumbling prayers under his breath. It was now possible to hear sounds of war in the distance. At least he thought he heard bombs and artillery. He realized he might have been imagining the rumbling sounds since he desired so strongly to see some sort of sign that the war was drawing to a close. He had heard no radio broadcasts for many months and relied on people like Corporal Linke to provide news about the progress of the war. As he glanced around the yard, Dietrich sensed unease among the guards and took that as a possible indication that things were not going well for the Fatherland.

Suddenly Linke was at his side. The corporal had been stealthier in his behavior since he and Dietrich had become friends of a sort. Whereas in the early days of his imprisonment Dietrich could expect a certain regularity to Linke's visits, lately the guard had been communicating with Dietrich at scattered and unpredictable times.

"Could I speak with you for a moment?" Linke whispered as he walked along beside Dietrich.

"Of course," Dietrich replied.

"There is an opening in the sick ward for an orderly," Linke said. "I thought you might be interested."

"Oh, is that so?" Dietrich answered, unsure of why he would want to be an orderly. But Linke quickly provided him with the details.

"There is a radio in the sick ward," Linke said, his voice returning to a whisper. "In the evenings, when the commandant and some of the other guards are either dining or drinking, we. . ."—and here his voice became so low that Dietrich had to put his head right next to Linke's in order to hear—". . .tune in to the BBC."

"The British? . . ." Dietrich began to ask, before he realized that he was talking above a whisper. There weren't any prisoners within twenty-five feet of them, but it was always wiser to be more cautious than was necessary.

"Yes," Linke responded. "We get what you might call a *different perspective* on the success stories fed to us by

German High Command broadcasts."

"I'm sure that you would," Dietrich said.

"But on a more personal level," Linke continued, "there are certain prisoners in the ward that would, I think, benefit from your presence."

"Oh?"

"Yes. As you know, there is very little to keep men from desiring death during these times. Sometimes I myself even think of death as a worthy option to continued existence under this regime. But I must admit that you have helped me to retain hope—not so much by your words as by your. . .demeanor. You seem to have an inner strength that all of us lack."

Dietrich didn't know what to say, and they walked in silence for a minute. Linke's words provoked in him a swell of conflicting emotions. He knew that, in part, he had been projecting a false image of strength in order to encourage his fellow prisoners. Yet another side of him had been growing spiteful toward their utter lack of humanity. It might have had something to do with his aristocratic upbringing, but he had always felt nothing but contempt for those who refused to take responsibility for their own lives—for those who had no respect that they had been created in the image of God.

"It's not so much that you are behaving like a saint," Linke continued. "My observation is that you have simply remained a somewhat normal human being, while the rest of us have long forgotten what *normal* is."

Dietrich was instantly humbled by Linke's words. Who was he to judge other men who lived on the edge of suicide every day, and who made conscious decisions to go on living every morning? Was it his place to be a judge, or a friend?

163

Besides, a long-dormant part of his heart had been rekindled during his conversation with Linke. It was the part of him that longed to be a pastor to those in need of a shepherd.

"I will gladly take the position in the sick ward," Dietrich finally responded. He looked up at Linke, who quickly suppressed a smile.

Linke said, "I knew you could not resist," as he turned on his heels and strode away toward the opposite end of the yard.

The sick ward was made up of a long room that was barely wider than a hallway and an adjoining smaller room. Beds lined the long room, and all of them were usually occupied. Some prisoners had obvious physical ailments—fever, severe rashes, wounds from beating or self-infliction— while the ailments of others were not so readily apparent. Yet the conditions of these latter patients seemed more tragic nonetheless. They lay still, or with a slight trembling in their limbs, eyes vacant and almost lifeless, skin cold to the touch. They were categorized as suffering from "extreme nervousness," Dietrich was told. The only care they received was a regular check of vital signs.

The smaller room contained a table and four chairs, a cabinet that stored the radio Linke had mentioned, a heater, and a coffeepot. An extremely tattered pack of playing cards graced the table.

Dietrich got along well with the other orderlies on his shift, though one of them held a deep resentment toward religion and the other was, from Dietrich's perspective, a weak-minded clod. Linke joined them most evenings to listen to the BBC broadcasts.

The chance to hear fairly objective news about the war

was eagerly anticipated by Dietrich, but he was soon discouraged by how slowly things were happening. The Allies had invaded Europe but were being thrown back again and again by desperate German troops. At times, Dietrich wished that they could use the radio to simply listen to some good, classical music—Bach or Beethoven, preferably.

When they weren't listening to the radio or playing cards, the orderlies spent time at the beds of the patients. Since card games were somewhat boring to Dietrich, he took on the bulk of the nursing duties. He performed these functions with the efficiency and care of a trained professional, though he often was only guessing as to the right thing to do.

He decided to view each patient as a parishioner, since as a pastor he had often been in the dark as to how to help his flock. He knew that it took the grace of God to penetrate to the core of a person's true infirmity. So he prayed over each patient on a daily basis, repeating fairly standard prayers that would cover a multitude of sins and sicknesses.

One patient, though, consistently resisted Dietrich's ministrations. Whenever Dietrich approached his bed, the man turned away. His wounds, primarily bruises to the head, were "officially" self-inflicted, and such self-abuse was indeed possible given that he had recently begun to refuse all food. But the stronger possibility was that he had been roughed up by some of the guards.

Dietrich found out from another orderly that the man's name was Sauter, that he was a Communist, and that he would probably be executed in the near future.

Dietrich prayed for the chance to talk to Sauter, and soon the opportunity was given. One day, as he passed his bed without stopping, Sauter surprisingly called out for him.

"What is your name?" the patient asked.

"Bonhoeffer," Dietrich answered.

"I've noticed how you stop at each bed to do your priestly duty."

"I am not a priest. I am only a man," Dietrich said.

"Still, you act like a priest," Sauter said.

"Maybe," Dietrich responded, not willing to get into an argument with a condemned man.

"Why do you waste your time praying for these animals? They certainly don't reciprocate your goodwill."

"I don't pray for them in order to gain their friendship," Dietrich answered.

"No, you feel it is your duty as a Christian," Sauter said flatly, without condescension.

"Something like that," Dietrich said, momentarily confused.

Sauter leaned over the edge of the bed and spat on the floor. "I think that men have invented the concept of duty in order to justify their vilest actions. My experience has told me that untold numbers of vicious and meaningless acts are done in the name of justice."

"I agree that duty has been used as an excuse for a multitude of sins," Dietrich replied, "but that does not mean that the concept of duty itself should be put away. Surely even you, as a Communist, feel a duty to something higher than mere self-interest."

Sauter laughed, and then his laughing turned to coughing. Dietrich went to a nearby sink and brought him back a glass of water.

"I do have a sense of duty toward certain principles," Sauter was finally able to say. "But they only have to do with making advances toward frauleins on a first date." Then he laughed again.

Dietrich smiled and said, "Well, at least that's a start."

Then Sauter's smile disappeared. "Have you ever seen one of your prayers answered?"

"One is being answered right now."

"Is that so?"

"Yes, I've wanted to speak with you for the past week, but I didn't want to force myself upon you. You were in obvious pain."

"More pain than you can imagine," Sauter said. Then he asked, "Did you want to convert me?"

Dietrich looked intently at the man's scarred face and could not help thinking that Jesus had been in the same place as Sauter two thousand years before. The suffering they both bore was more similar than different.

"Conversion was not really on my mind," Dietrich said truthfully. "I simply wanted to help you in your suffering if I could. Besides, I cannot help to convert someone who does not want to be converted. I just assumed that you did not."

"Ah, a dangerous assumption, is it not, Bonhoeffer?" Sauter said, smiling as well as he could. "Are you sure you want to play so fast and loose with my eternal soul?" The sarcasm seemed to be taking a lot of energy out of Sauter. He sank deeper into his pillow and said, "But in any case, you were correct."

Dietrich simply nodded.

"You know that they are probably going to stand me against a wall sometime soon, don't you, Bonhoeffer?"

After a pause, Dietrich said, "I hear a lot of things, but I don't know which rumors to believe."

"Oh, you can be sure that the Nazis are going to take as many Communists with them as they can before the Allies wipe us all out." Then he added, "They will probably get rid of all the rogue priests, too."

Dietrich smiled at the show of spirit in the suffering man. "Well then, we have something in common, don't we?" he said.

"Yes," Sauter said, now deadly serious. "We are both supporters of lost causes."

Dietrich brooded on his conversation with Sauter for several days. The young Communist would not speak to him again except for the most banal of exchanges, though he did allow Dietrich to pray over him, which Dietrich took as a sign of hope.

What really bothered Dietrich about Sauter was that his attitudes were eerily close to his own. His own experiences were causing him to reevaluate once again his conception of the Church, and of the responsibility of the individual Christian in the modern, self-sufficient world. Obviously the twentieth-century Church had already failed in many areas. What failures lay ahead, and how could they be avoided, Dietrich wondered. He also mused on whether the Church needed to be radically changed in order to meet the challenges of a world that seemed to shun the very institution.

A week later, Sauter was executed in the yard of the prison.

Afterward, Dietrich's thinking took on a new intensity, and he found himself deeply mourning Sauter's death. He did not feel bad simply because Sauter had not accepted Christianity. After all, the man had grown up in a world in which Christianity had been presented to him in irrelevant terms that any honest and intelligent person could quite reasonably reject. Sauter had found Christianity to be *merely* a form of religion and, as such, dispensable.

Dietrich determined that he had little to say to people like Sauter if he approached them from a traditionally religious point of view. These nonreligious people could not make a connection between what they saw of religion and what they were seeing in the world. Thus they turned to Communism or Fascism, two ideologies that seemed to confront the world on its own terms and tried to make a difference.

In a series of letters that would shake the theological world when they were later published, Dietrich began to lay out his thoughts on this subject in letters to his good friend Eberhard Bethge. These letters began to be written in April of 1944 and continued throughout the summer. In the first Dietrich wrote the following:

You would be surprised, and perhaps even worried, by my theological thoughts and the conclusions they lead to; and this is where I miss you most of all, because I don't know anyone else with whom I could so well discuss them to have my thinking clarified. What is bothering me incessantly is the question of what Christianity really is, or indeed who Christ really is, for us today. The time when people could be told everything by means of words, whether theological or pious, is over, and so is the time of inwardness and conscience—and that means the time of religion in general. We are moving towards a completely religionless time; people as they are now simply cannot be religious anymore. Even those who honestly describe themselves as "religious" do not in the least act up to it, and so they presumably mean something quite different by "religious."[1]

Since 1933, Dietrich had been continually troubled by the ability of Nazism to gain a stronghold in the highly religious country of Germany. Throughout the intervening years, the thought began to occur to him on a regular basis that perhaps Germany was just that—religious, but not necessarily wholly Christian. As he now took the opportunity to develop these thoughts in prison, he surmised that all people down through history were naturally religious. That religiousness took many forms, one of which was Christianity. But were "religion" and its forms absolutely necessary to Christianity and the truth of the gospel? And what happened when human beings, in defiance of their long history, suddenly decided that being religious was not worthwhile or tenable anymore? Could Christianity survive in a "religionless" world? He wrote to Bethge:

> *How can Christ become the Lord of the religionless as well? Are there religionless Christians? If religion is only a garment of Christianity—and even this garment has looked very different at different times—then what is religionless Christianity?*[2]

Dietrich extended his thinking to take in the question of why people became religious at all. He came to the conclusion that most became religious in order to find answers to unanswered questions. This was reasonable enough, he supposed, yet it put religion in a vulnerable position. For what happened when science began to provide the answers to the previously unanswerable questions? Did that not mean that religion would simply be pushed to the sidelines? Dietrich thought that that was exactly what had happened in the twentieth century. Since people had been religious only in order to make sense of mysteries, when those mysteries had been solved, religion was no longer necessary. Those people who remained religious then clung to a God who was basically irrelevant, and it made them look silly to the world.

But if God could be liberated from outdated "religious" conceptions of Him, His true relevance as Creator and Lord could then perhaps be revealed. Dietrich explored these ideas in a further letter.

While I'm often reluctant to mention God by name to religious people—because that name somehow seems to me here not to ring true, and I feel myself to be slightly dishonest (it's particularly bad when others start to talk in religious jargon; I then dry up almost completely and feel awkward and uncomfortable)—to people with no religion I can on occasion mention Him by name quite calmly and as a matter of course. Religious people speak of God when human knowledge (perhaps because they are too lazy to think) has come to an end, or when human resources fail— in fact it is always the deus ex machina that they bring on to the scene, either for the apparent solution of insoluble problems, or as strength in human failure—always, that is to say, exploiting human weakness or human boundaries. . . . It always seems to me that we are trying anxiously in this way to reserve some space for God; I should like to speak of God not on the boundaries but at the center, not in weakness but in strength;

and therefore not in death and guilt but in man's
life and goodness.... God's "beyond" is not the
beyond of our cognitive faculties.... God is
beyond in the midst of our life. The church
stands, not at the boundaries where human pow-
ers give out, but in the midst of the village.[3]

To Dietrich, a God who only existed to "fill in the gaps" of our knowledge was susceptible of turning into a pagan god, which is exactly what had happened in Germany under the Nazis. A limited God was a God who could be adapted for human purposes. But if God was God at all, thought Dietrich, He should also be relevant in those areas where humankind had found itself capable of carrying on without Him. His presence should be ever-present, not just something to fall back upon in times of failure. He should be capable of being the Lord of all creation, and of all human activities. In late May, Dietrich wrote:

Weizsacker's book The World-View of Physics *is*
still keeping me very busy. It has again brought
home to me quite clearly how wrong it is to use
God as a stop-gap for the incompleteness of our
knowledge. If in fact the frontiers of knowledge
are being pushed further and further back (and
that is bound to be the case), then God is being
pushed back with them, and is therefore continu-
ally in retreat. We are to find God in what we
know, not in what we don't know; God wants us to
realize His presence, not in unsolved problems but
in those that are solved. That is true of the rela-
tionship between God and scientific knowledge,

but it is also true of the wider human problems of death, suffering, and guilt. It is now possible to find, even for these questions, human answers that take no account whatever of God. In point of fact, people deal with these questions without God (it has always been so), and it is simply not true to say that only Christianity has the answers to them. As to the idea of "solving" problems, it may be that the Christian answers are just as unconvincing—or convincing—as any others. Here again, God is no stop-gap; He must be recognized at the center of life, not when we are at the end of our resources; it is His will to be recognized in life, and not only when death comes; in health and vigor, and not only in suffering; in our activities, and not only in sin. The ground for this lies in the revelation of God in Jesus Christ. He is the center of life, and He certainly didn't "come" to answer our unsolved problems. From the center of life certain questions, and their answers, are seen to be wholly irrelevant (I'm thinking of the judgment pronounced on Job's friends). In Christ there are no [merely] "Christian problems."[4]

It is easy to misunderstand these statements. Dietrich, of course, was writing them as private thoughts to be shared with a friend. Bethge later made them public only when he saw their worth as a critique of what Dietrich was calling "religion."

Basically, Dietrich was recognizing that people in "Christian lands" were susceptible to distortions of the gospel message because of their natural proclivity to be religious. Being religious did not make someone a Christian, although a religious person was likely to believe he was a Christian if that was the dominant form of religious expression in his culture. He might be thoroughly pagan, or, in other words, "merely religious." To make an analogy, Christianity for them was like bullfighting in Spain. They entered into the spirit of the crowd (or the culture) without understanding what they were doing, or why they were doing it.

In Dietrich's mind, such "Christians" were living according to a mythological reality, not a biblical reality. Like pagans in all cultures, they believed in a redemption myth, or a story about an ultimate deliverer, but they didn't understand the decisive difference of the biblical story. In one of Dietrich's last letters on the topic of "religionless Christianity," he wrote about this issue:

The difference between the Christian hope of resurrection and the mythological hope is that the former sends a man back to his life on earth in a wholly new way which is even more sharply defined than it is in the Old Testament. The Christian, unlike the devotees of the redemption myths, has no last line of escape available from earthly tasks and difficulties into the eternal, but, like Christ Himself ("My God, why hast Thou forsaken Me?"), he must drink the earthly cup to the dregs, and only in his doing so is the crucified and risen Lord with him, and he crucified and risen with Christ. This world must not be prematurely written off; in this the Old and New Testaments are at one. Redemption myths arise from human

boundary-experiences, but Christ takes hold of a
man at the center of his life.[5]

Much of Dietrich's thinking in these letters had been influenced by his continual reading of the Old Testament. The injunction against reading the Old Testament that had been passed down by the Reich Church had sent him back to the Bible with a fervor. During his first year at Tegel, he read it all the way through three times. What he found was that the Old Testament, which could not easily be separated from the message of the New Testament, was all about living by faith in *this* world. It was not about holding on until another world appeared. And if someone was required to live by faith here, he could not be irresponsible about what happened here. He could not be lackadaisical about, or withdraw in piety from, any sphere of life. To retreat from life, to Dietrich, was to retreat from a full, biblical vision of who God was.

The message of the gospel, when taken in conjunction with the Old Testament, was that Christ had come in the flesh to reveal the life of God in all its aspects. The Incarnation showed God's respect for human life and His own physical creation. It was not merely a redemption myth; it was a vision of reality. Christ was the man who had not only died for others, but who *lived* for them, as well.

nineteen

Study of Ethics

Dietrich was reading James's Epistle when the first blackout occurred. It surprised him to be plunged into soupy darkness suddenly, but unlike most of the prisoners, he had been expecting it. From listening to the BBC, he knew that Berlin was no longer out of range of Allied bombers. He thus had a better sense that the net was closing, that the Nazi war machine was winding down, and that Hitler and his henchmen were running out of places to hide.

Corporal Linke suddenly appeared out of the dark with a small lantern in his hand. He took a large key and unlocked Dietrich's cell door.

"Come, Bonhoeffer," he said in a knowing voice. "We are all going down to the yard."

"The yard?"

"It is difficult for the walls to collapse on us if only the stars are above us," Linke responded, with a slight smile creasing his lips.

"Do you believe there is any chance that the bombing

will reach us tonight?" Dietrich asked as he arose from his creaky chair.

"Probably not tonight, but who knows?" Linke said with a shrug. "Nothing is predictable anymore."

When Dietrich joined a dozen other prisoners on the walkway, he could discern the fear and tension on their faces, even in the flickering lantern light. The man in front of him was trembling, and Dietrich placed a hand on his shoulder to steady him. When he did this, the man instantly spun around. His eyes were like those of a crazed animal, and Dietrich quickly realized that the man was quaking with fear. He was probably under the conviction that they were all being led down to the yard for execution.

"It's all right, Friend," Dietrich said calmly. "It is only another drill. The military people around here are quite fond of drills, I'm afraid."

The man blinked uncomprehendingly. He had dark, close-cropped hair and a dense stubble of whiskers on his pointy chin. His cheeks were drawn in from hunger, and his shoulders were rounded. Dietrich wondered what supposed "crime" against the Nazis had brought the man to this place of misery. It was enough to make him welcome the inevitable bombing, since it would mean that the end of such suffering was at hand. Yet he knew that the bombs would create suffering, too.

Dietrich squeezed the man's shoulder tighter and looked into his eyes. "I promise you," he said, "that you will be safe tonight."

And for a moment, a softness that signaled the presence of a human spirit flashed across the man's eyes. The fear was suddenly absent from them. Then it was too dark to see anymore, and all of the men stumbled down to the yard together.

When, for several weeks, the blackouts came to occur every three or four days, the tension in the prison decreased. The blackouts were simply part of the routine, yet an unnecessary caution as bombs failed to fall on the city.

Most days, Dietrich worked on his study of ethics. The subject had increasingly fascinated him over the past decade, especially as he was thrust into positions where the ethical mandate was not so clear. He was glad, in a way, to have an opportunity to clarify his thoughts.

The overriding theme of the study had to do with how Christians should act under extreme conditions. Dietrich's own situation gave him ample opportunity to reflect on this topic, and to test his conclusions. Although in many ways he was simply continuing the thoughts that he expressed in *The Cost of Discipleship*, this book was written from the standpoint of someone who had been involved in a conspiracy against the leader of the state, an act that most Christians would consider to be unethical.

Before he answered the ultimate question of how an ethical person could justify rebellion against the government, though, he reiterated a few basic and vital points. He referred again to the *attitude* of obedience that Jesus commanded in the Sermon on the Mount, one that did not acknowledge any loyalties above or equal to one's loyalty to Christ. He also emphasized that obedience consisted in acting, rather than just believing, and that being "religious" was in no way the same as fulfilling one's responsibility as a Christian. A man's true responsibility, as Dietrich put it in his own unique way, was to be conformed to Christ, and thus to be everything that God had created him to be.

This was a simple doctrine, but it served its purpose by standing in direct contrast to the prevalent German ideal of the "superman." The superman was the man who transcended his own humanity and became semidivine through heroic action. Dietrich stated:

> *To be conformed with the Incarnate—that is to be a real man. It is man's right and duty that he should be a man. The quest for the superman, the pursuit of the heroic, the cult of the demigod, all this is not the proper concern of man, for it is untrue. The real man is not an object either for contempt or for dei-fication, but an object of the love of God. . . . The real man is at liberty to be his creator's creature. To be conformed with the Incarnate is to have the right to be the man one really is. Now there is no more pretense, no more hypocrisy or self-violence, no more compulsion to be something other, better, and more ideal than what one is. God loves the real man. God became a real man.*[1]

In his *Ethics*, Dietrich also went beyond *The Cost of Discipleship* in his statements about the treatment of the Jews. His concern for German Jews developed in the late 1920s when segregation first began. He had seen the effects of the Aryan Clause on normal, hardworking families. He remembered the example of his Grandmother Tafel, who in the early 1930s had defied a cordon of soldiers and walked through their ranks in order to shop at a Jewish establish-ment. He had been in Berlin when *Kristallnacht* occurred. He had learned about the concentration camps from Hans. And he had helped his own sister escape from Germany under cover of night in 1939.

Dietrich reminded his readers that Jesus Himself had been a Jew, and that the New Testament was not understand-able apart from its Jewish context. He went even further by saying that the despised Jews were actually the "least of these" that Jesus spoke about in the Gospels, and that by deporting them to the camps, the Nazis were, in effect, deporting Christ. Then he went on to blame the churches for not speaking out against the camps, declaring that German Christians were partially guilty for the deaths and ruined lives of a countless number of helpless Jews. It was strong language, but to Dietrich it was the unadulterated truth.

The most complex part of the book, though, had to do with his attempt to reconcile his Christianity with his involvement in the assassination plots against Hitler. But to understand his reasoning, one has to understand first his convictions about discipleship.

The first thing he did was to try to "demystify" patriotism by pointing out its falsity when seen as a more important or relevant responsibility than one's discipleship under Christ. He asserted that if patriotism, as a lesser responsibility, was not placed under the larger responsibility of discipleship, it led to a perversion of human character and a lessening of respect for individual life itself. This meant that the commands of the state were always subject to Christ's judgment. When the Church itself confused these two responsibilities, and placed country before Christ, it abdicated its spiritual authority. All true Christians then had a mandate to resist such a "Church."

Furthermore, if the government demanded that Christians sign away their submission to Christ in order to serve the state, Christians had the responsibility to resist that government absolutely. Under a biblical view, such a government was a false one, in that it was not operating within the sphere God intended. To serve that type of government was never an act of patriotism, and was probably a sin.

The next part of the book was even more complicated as Dietrich attempted to justify not only resistance, but actual violence against the leader of an illegitimate government. At no point did Dietrich ever state that such violence was not a sin. He never implied that the assassin and his accomplices were not guilty, that they weren't under the judgment of God. Indeed, they were to be considered "bloody men," like King David in the Bible.

Yet for Dietrich, the other options carried an even greater weight of guilt. For him, failure to act was simply irresponsible. He who refused to get involved placed his "innocence" above the needs of the people. Dietrich declared that the Church had too long been only interested in maintaining a righteousness like that of the Pharisees. For too long it had been concerned only with keeping its hands clean, even to the point of failing to face facts. Dietrich thought that such an "otherworldly" Christianity was a denial of the Incarnation, and that God Himself had entered into the world in order to save it.

In one of his most radical theological statements, Dietrich said that Christ Himself had entered into a "fellowship of guilt" in order to save those who could not save themselves.[2] He said that Christ did not do this in an abstract, symbolic way. He actually did take the sin and guilt of the world upon His shoulders. His flesh-and-blood body actually did die upon a sinner's cross. And Christ did this because there was no other way. So if Christians made up the body of Christ upon earth, Dietrich continued, how could they expect to get by with any less of a sacrifice?

In his eyes, a concern for self-preservation was directly contrary to discipleship, though it was not necessarily contrary to religion.

181

twenty

The Questioning

Franz Sonderegger was a thin, bespectacled man who always sat ramrod straight in his chair. As he took his job seriously, he was determined to find out whether the Abwehr had been carrying out legitimate counterintelligence activities or, as was suspected, undermining Germany's war efforts.

Dietrich was unsure what information Sonderegger possessed, but he knew that Hans's portfolio, containing evidence regarding the concentration camps and other Nazi war crimes, was still hidden among the Abwehr's huge compilation of files. Hans had not wanted to destroy it in case a coup succeeded, but now that they had all been arrested, the portfolio was, in effect, their death certificate. It was only a matter of time before somebody found it and made the obvious connections.

Still, Dietrich held out hope that in the space of time before the portfolio was found something dramatic could happen. Though remote, there was still a chance that Hitler might be eliminated and an alternative government established. If that happened, it would be the fulfillment of his and Hans's goals and plans. It was also possible that Dietrich might free himself on a technicality, since he had not yet been formally charged with a serious crime.

All in all, he was hopeful, while remaining realistic.

Sonderegger met with Dietrich every ten days or so in a dusty, narrow office with pale green walls. It was a room that seemed to be designed to induce nausea.

The questioning always followed a predictable pattern, and Dietrich's anxiety about his sessions with Sonderegger grew less as time passed. The preparation that he and Hans had done while anticipating their arrest had paid off. They had collaborated on a defense that painted the Abwehr's most questionable activities as, in actuality, their most clever maneuvers. In other words, when the Abwehr looked like a traitorous organization was when its members were carrying out their prescribed duties most imaginatively.

Dietrich and Hans believed it was a technique that would, ironically, confound their unimaginative foes. And so far their prediction had turned out to be correct. Sonderegger seemed to grow more frustrated and desperate as the weeks went by, especially as the war kept taking turns for the worse, as seen from the Nazi perspective.

The investigator usually began the sessions by questioning Dietrich's commitment to the Third Reich. Many times, this took the form of suspecting his motives for joining the Abwehr rather than the regular military.

Sonderegger: "Do you ever suffer pangs of guilt for not risking your life on the front lines with most other German men of your age?"

Dietrich: "There are many reasons why I was denied that privilege. Much of it had to do with timing and thus was out of my control."

Sonderegger: "Timing, eh? Do you mean that military call-up would have put a damper on all your travel plans? You certainly were on the move in the early days of the war. Or do you mean that military training would have upset the idyllic times spent relaxing at. . .what is this? A Catholic monastery? Quite a place to find a Lutheran pastor!"

Dietrich: "Yes, I was at a Benedictine monastery, but you must remember that I had been banned from pastoring in the German Church at that time. I was an agent of the Abwehr and nothing else. My supervisors did not have immediate plans for me and even suggested that I hole up at a remote place until I was called upon. Their reasoning was murky to me, but I did not complain. I must confess that I used the time to work on scattered theological writings that I had left undone."

Sonderegger: "How convenient."

Dietrich: "Yes, it was. But as you mentioned, there were also breaks in my "idyllic relaxation" when I was able to do a bit of traveling—mainly to establish relationships that would later be useful."

Sonderegger: "Relationships in England and Sweden?"

Dietrich: "In counterespionage, the most important relationships one has are with the enemy."

Sonderegger: "Bonhoeffer, please do not lecture me on counterespionage."

Dietrich: "My apologies, Herr Sonderegger."

During one session, Sonderegger surprised Dietrich by asking, "Didn't Martin Luther himself say that a Christian should always support and obey the governing authorities that are set over him?"

Dietrich was fully aware of the irony in Sonderegger's attempt to use Luther against him. "He said the Christian should obey, but that worship was out of the question," he replied.

"Oh, so you believe that our Führer is requiring the German people to worship him instead of God?"

Dietrich tensed. These questions were taking him into uncharted waters. Direct questions about his feelings toward the Führer had to be handled delicately. "I simply feel that a Christian has the responsibility to serve his country to the best of his ability, which is all that his country can ask of him," he finally answered.

"Clever, Bonhoeffer," Sonderegger replied. "But I am curious about your specific feelings toward the Third Reich."

Dietrich knew that any blanket endorsement of the Nazi regime on his part would be seen as disingenuous since he was on public record as an early critic of Hitler. "Like any responsible citizen, I look at the state of public life with a critical eye and think about how things could be made better," he said. "But once the course of our destiny seemed unchangeable, I threw myself wholeheartedly into the service of my country."

"You say *my country* with a tinge of bitterness in your voice," Sonderegger said, "as if you believed that *your country* had been despoiled."

Dietrich was tempted to let all of his true feelings spill out at that moment, but he had been trained too well by Hans to allow that to happen. "No, I still have a great deal of pride in, and hope for, my country. I pray for it every day."

Sonderegger slid down in his chair, which was entirely uncharacteristic, and touched his fingertips together in front of his mouth. "If I were not afraid of the answer, I would question you about the content of your prayers," he said softly. "Maybe they would give me greater insight into your inner motives than your answers are providing."

Dietrich could not contain a small smile. "I think that your instincts are probably correct on that point, Herr Sonderegger, but the longer I live, the more I believe that God alone knows a man's heart." Then he added, "And God alone is able to *judge* that heart."

Sonderegger sighed. "Yes, Bonhoeffer. It would help if I could put God on the witness stand. . . ." His voice trailed off. Then he waved his hand dismissively in the air, collected his satchel, and left the room.

twenty-one

Death Warrant

On July 20, 1944, Colonel Count Claus Schenk von Stauffenburg walked into a conference room where Hitler was meeting with his top military personnel. He was carrying a briefcase that contained a bomb on a timer. Von Stauffenburg avoided a search because he was a well-known officer and had lost his right forearm and an eye at the front. He was trusted. At some point during the meeting, von Stauffenburg placed the briefcase at Hitler's feet and then excused himself to leave for the airport. As he was driving away, he heard the bomb explode. He smiled, confident that Hitler was dead.

But Hitler was not dead. After von Stauffenburg left the room, another officer had unsuspectingly moved the briefcase. When the bomb exploded, four officers who were sitting around the conference table were killed, while Hitler himself escaped with only minor injuries. Later that day, the Führer spoke about how Providence had spared him. He also vowed revenge against the conspirators.

Sitting in his cell at Tegel, Dietrich heard the news reports about this latest, and last, attempt on Hitler's life. Over the next few weeks, he would also hear about the executions of von Stauffenburg and General Beck, the Abwehr chief who had been linked to the assassination attempt in the course of the ensuing investigation. This meant that the noose was tightening around anyone connected to the Abwehr. And when the Gestapo discovered, at around the same time, hidden papers about the plot at the Abwehr's air-raid shelter, Dietrich's death warrant was effectively signed.

After that, the only thing keeping him alive was the Gestapo's desire to gather as much information as it could about the conspiracy. His only hope for survival was a quick end to the war. If the war ended abruptly, it might cause so much confusion that his potential executioners would flee from the Allies before carrying out their appointed task. Though all of the contingencies were perfectly clear to Dietrich, nobody would have thought, just by looking at him, that he was under any stress at all. His intense devotional life, even in prison, had allowed him to gain a sense of peace concerning the future.

Many of his fellow prisoners who survived the war would later recall Dietrich's peaceful demeanor during this time and remark on how calm he was. They would remember how encouraging he was to those who were better off than he, and how resolute he was in his simple faith toward God. In the worst of all possible circumstances, it seemed that he had resigned himself to God's will and had found an inward contentment.

This is not to say that this time was not difficult for Dietrich. He was still human, after all, and had a deep desire to live. But he had matured through his experiences and had arrived at a place of trust and spiritual freedom that probably could not have been attained otherwise. There were only two things that he worried about on a consistent basis: first, whether he could undergo torture without betraying his friends, and second, how his possible death would affect his family and Maria.

One day Dietrich sat in his cell and composed a poem about his newfound sense of freedom in captivity. The poem was entitled "Stations on the Road to Freedom" and was broken into four sections:

Discipline

If you set out to seek freedom, then learn above
    all discipline of soul and senses, so that your
    passions and your limbs might not lead you
    confusedly hither and yon.
Chaste be your spirit and body, subject to your
    own will, and obedient to seek out the goal
    that they have been given.
No one discovers the secret of freedom but
    through self-control.

Action

Dare to do what is just, not what fancy may
    call for;
Lose no time with what may be, but boldly grasp
    what is real.
The world of thought is escape; freedom comes
    only through action.
Step out beyond anxious waiting and into the storm
    of events, carried only by God's command and

189

by your own faith; then will freedom exultantly
cry out to welcome your spirit.

Suffering

Wondrous transformation! Your strong and active
hands are tied now. Powerless, alone, you see
the end of your action.
Still, you take a deep breath and lay your struggle
for justice, quietly and in faith, into a mightier
hand.
Just for one blissful moment, you tasted the
sweetness of freedom, then you handed it over
to God, that He might make it whole.

Death

Come now, highest moment on the road to freedom eternal,
Death, put down the ponderous chains and
demolish the walls of our mortal bodies,
the walls of our blinded souls, that we might
finally see what mortals have kept us from
seeing.
Freedom, how long we have sought you through
discipline, action, and suffering.
Dying, now we behold your face in the counte-
nance of God.[1]

On October 8, Dietrich was transferred from Tegel to a
Gestapo prison in downtown Berlin. All of his communication with the outside world (except for two Christmas letters, one to his mother and one to Maria) was cut off at this

point, and he suffered under almost constant interrogation. Airraid sirens went off at all hours of the day and night, and the prisoners were constantly shuffled back and forth between their cells and an airraid bunker.

On one of his trips back to his cell, Dietrich noticed an emaciated man lying on a cot in an open cell down the hall from his own. Though the man looked much different from the last time he had seen him, Dietrich recognized Hans immediately. The next time the prisoners filed back from the bunker, he ducked into the cell where Hans lay. In the fatigue and dreariness of those days, nobody seemed to notice.

Dietrich crouched next to Hans's cot and took stock of his friend's physical condition. His brother-in-law's face looked like a death mask, with his eyes and lips having receded back into his skull. His eyes also seemed to be crusted shut. At first, Dietrich thought that Hans was actually dead, but then he noticed the shallow movement of his thin chest.

"Hans, can you hear me?" he whispered.

There was no response, and he said it again, louder.

Finally, Hans's eyes, with a supreme effort, flickered open. They were milky and unfocused. "Dietrich?" he rasped.

"Yes, it is Dietrich. Oh, Hans, is there anything I can do for you?"

Almost imperceptibly, Hans shook his head. Dietrich felt hot tears welling up in his own eyes.

"Hans, I want you to know," he said, "that I have not betrayed us. I have not given them anything that might condemn us. You taught me well."

Hans merely blinked, but in that blink Dietrich thought that he discerned a gesture of approval. Dietrich ran his

191

fingers through Hans's stringy hair and wiped his brow with his handkerchief. Then he slipped back to his own cell undetected.

The next evening, Dietrich saw that Hans was not in his cell anymore. After frantically questioning one of the guards, he was informed that the Gestapo had taken him to a hospital for treatment. "They want to get a few more words out of him before they shoot him," the surly guard explained.

The next morning during his daily interrogation session, Dietrich at first refused to speak. With Hans gone, he felt some of his own strength slipping away, and he did not trust himself to say all the right things. But his obstinance was not going over well with Keltenbrunner, the senior Gestapo agent who was questioning him in place of Sonderegger, who had proved ineffective. At one point, Keltenbrunner slammed his pen down and approached Dietrich in a threatening manner.

"Do you know, Bonhoeffer," he hissed, "that I can have your beloved parents and fiancée put to death this very day?"

This threat caused Dietrich's breath to catch in his throat. He finally managed to say, "I am always ready to answer your questions. Please forgive me. I am merely tired."

"That's better," Keltenbrunner said, settling back into his chair. "But since you are so weary today, I only have one question of any importance to ask you."

"Yes?" Dietrich whispered.

Keltenbrunner pulled three separate sheets of paper out of his satchel and laid them on the table in front of Dietrich. Dietrich could not read the dense script on them through his bleary eyes.

"Do you know what these are?" the Gestapo agent asked.

Dietrich shook his head.

"This is a set of detailed confessions regarding your

activities against the state. My single question for you this morning is whether you are willing to sign them." The agent paused for a moment. "They are really just a formality, of course."

Dietrich sighed. "I have no reason to sign them now, do I? I cannot stop you from forging my signature on them yourself."

"Quite right," Keltenbrunner replied. "But I would rather not have to do that. I prefer to do everything with your full cooperation."

"And I believe that I have given it."

Keltenbrunner laughed out loud. "Don't insult me, Bonhoeffer."

At this, Dietrich sat straight in his chair. He had finally grown tired of the abuse. His face grew red as he said, "If you can show me any hard evidence that I have been disloyal to my country, I want you to show it to me now." His voice was trembling. "Because I certainly cannot remember a single time in your very thorough investigation that you or your comrades have turned up anything worthy of keeping me here in this death pit, away from my family and friends for another Christmas. I have been very forthright in answering your questions. If you are still not satisfied, it must either be because I am innocent, or because you are too stupid to ask the right questions." He was incensed and could not stop himself. "I will repeat what I have said all along. Everything that I have done since the beginning of the war has been related either to legitimate counterespionage or to my work as a minister of Christ. If those two activities meshed in such a way as to cause suspicion, I can only say that these are very strange and confusing times in which it is quite easy to misinterpret the actions of even the most honest of citizens."

Dietrich then slumped back into his chair, exhausted. He noticed that Keltenbrunner's ears were red, and that there was a good chance that he might be shot in the next few seconds.

But Keltenbrunner merely replied, "You are correct about one thing, Bonhoeffer. Today *is* Christmas."

Over the next month, Dietrich tried to keep from despairing. His sense of inner peace was wavering. It would have been even more difficult if he hadn't been helped by the presence of an unexpected friend, Fabian von Schlabrendorff, a cousin of Maria's. Von Schlabrendorff knew a lot about Dietrich and could sympathize with his plight. Dietrich told him about Maria's letters and about the awful interrogations. They also discussed all the possible scenarios for the end of the war and the reconstruction of Germany. Dietrich struck von Schlabrendorff as someone who remained hopeful about the future but who was also resigned entirely to the will of God. Dietrich's more complicated inner feelings remained private.

They didn't talk much about theology since von Schlabrendorff had never studied it, but Dietrich's simple devotion to Christ still showed through in his speech and demeanor—and that he complained less than anyone. One evening, after they had run out of things to talk about, Dietrich passed a slip of paper across to von Schlabrendorff's cell.

"This is my testimony," he said simply.

Von Schlabrendorff looked at the piece of paper. It was a poem entitled "Who Am I?" and was dated June 1944.

Who am I? They often tell me
I would step from my cell's confinement
calmly, cheerfully, firmly,
like a squire from his country house.

Who am I? They often tell me
I would talk to my warders
freely and friendly and clearly,
as though it were mine to command.

Who am I? They also tell me
I would bear the days of misfortune
equably, smilingly, proudly,
like one accustomed to win.

Am I then really all that which other men tell of?
Or am I only what I know of myself,
restless and longing and sick, like a bird in a cage,
struggling for breath, as though hands were com-
    pressing my throat,
yearning for colors, for flowers, for the voices of
    birds,
thirsting for words of kindness, for neighborliness,
trembling with anger at despotisms and petty
    humiliation,
tossing in expectation of great events,
powerlessly trembling for friends at an infinite
    distance,
weary and empty at praying, at thinking, at making,
faint, and ready to say farewell to it all?

Who am I? This or the other?
Am I one person today, and tomorrow another?
am I both at once? A hypocrite before others,
and before myself a contemptibly woebegone
    weakling?
Or is something within me still like a beaten army,
fleeing in disorder from victory already achieved?

195

Who am I? They mock me, these lonely questions
     of mine.
Whoever I am, Thou knowest, O God, I am thine.[2]

On February 7, Dietrich learned that he was being transferred to Buchenwald concentration camp. Before he was
taken away, he gave von Schlabrendorff his only copy of *The
Cost of Discipleship*. And when the German aristocrat was
released after the war to find that his once spacious home
had been reduced to rubble by Allied bombs, this book was
his only real possession besides the clothes on his back.

Buchenwald, which had already grown notorious within
Germany as an efficient death camp, was oppressive, both
spiritually and physically. Dietrich was kept in the section
where officers were held, both "traitorous" Germans and
Allied prisoners of war. At first he was alone in a cell, but
soon he was joined by General von Rabenau, a fellow
conspirator.

As the two men talked, Dietrich was surprised and
pleased to learn that the general had taken a theological
degree at Bonn University in his younger days. This meant
that Dietrich had someone to talk to about his private
meditations. These thoughts had remained cramped in his
brain for so long that when he began talking, they rushed
out in a torrent. But von Rabenau was able to give as good
as he got, and the two men often argued good-naturedly
much of the night about theological issues that Dietrich
studied all of his adult life.

During the day, interrogations continued. Again, these
were the sole reason he was still alive. Hitler, even as the
Allies surrounded Berlin, wanted to root out every last traitor to his regime.

Overhearing Dietrich and von Rabenau's conversations through the dividing wall of their cells was Captain Payne Best of the British Secret Service, who had been captured in the early days of the war. By February of 1945, Best was a cynical man and an atheist, but he understood enough German to appreciate the energetic discussions between the two theologians. Still, he often wondered how men could be so concerned about the proper meanings of the sacraments in times like those.

When all of the prisoners were taken into the communal showers during air raids, Best himself started conversations with Dietrich, who could speak a rough English on account of his sojourns in London and New York.

"It's quite heartening to hear the British howitzers off in the distance, isn't it?" Best said one time.

"Yes, quite," Dietrich responded. "It almost causes me to get my hopes up."

"Well, they really are our only hope, aren't they?"

"Not our only hope," Dietrich said slyly, "but then I've always had a hard time placing my trust in pieces of cold, hard steel."

"But that's what war is about nowadays, Bonhoeffer. Cold, hard steel. I'm afraid it's not a very human affair."

"I completely agree."

Best lit a cigarette and said, "I know you are a religious man, Bonhoeffer—"

Dietrich tried to interrupt, but Best continued. "I must confess that I cannot claim this about myself. Not to offend, but it would be almost obscene for me to believe in God after all I have seen."

After a pause, Dietrich said softly, "I understand what you are saying. It has greatly disturbed me that men who claimed to be religious started all of this. In fact, it sickens

197

me. But I prefer to believe that God is the reality that stands outside of this unreality."

"Are you saying that the war isn't real?" Best shot back, incredulous.

"I'm sorry, I don't mean to sound like a mystic," Dietrich said. "All I am saying is that the war is a farce—it is a farce and repudiation of all that God intended for humankind. Though He can accomplish His purposes through it—simply because He is God—the war is not His will and He cannot be blamed for it. Again, I apologize. My theological training has not taught me how to speak clearly."

"No, I think I see what you are saying," Best said, puffing on his cigarette. "I just think that it takes a whole lot of faith to believe in something like that."

"I hope it doesn't take too much," Dietrich said, smiling. "Then none of us could measure up."

After the war, Best would write a book about his experiences as a prisoner of war. He did not have very good things to say about most of his fellow prisoners, but about Dietrich he wrote the following:

> *Bonhoeffer was all humility and sweetness; he always seemed to diffuse an atmosphere of happiness, of joy in every smallest event in life, and of deep gratitude for the mere fact of being alive. There was something doglike in the look of fidelity in his eyes and his gladness if you showed that you liked him. He was one of the very few men I ever met to whom his God was real and ever close to him.*[3]

On Easter Day, April 1, 1945, guards came through the corridors shouting for the prisoners to get ready. They would be leaving Buchenwald that day and possibly heading out on foot. One of the prisoners shouted out, "Are we going to be shot in the woods?" But his question went unanswered.

Dietrich and von Rabenau gathered their meager belongings and stuffed them into small rucksacks. An eerie silence pervaded the corridors after the guards went out, as if the prisoners were not ready to say any final words to one another.

Then the guards came back and told the men to file outside.

"Where are we going?" one asked.

"A truck has been found. You will be going south" was the answer.

The prisoners' relief at knowing they were not going to be taken into the woods was replaced by a dread of what "going south" might mean, for it was well known that the infamous "annihilation camp" at Flossenburg was in that direction. Nobody went to Flossenburg to serve out a lengthy sentence.

As the prisoners lined up outside, they heard the sounds of heavy artillery in the near distance. They also heard the guards discussing matters worriedly among themselves, not hiding their determination to save themselves and let the prisoners go should they be overtaken.

That meant there was hope.

Dietrich and the others climbed into the heavy lorry, a behemoth of a machine that was powered by a wood-burning generator. The prisoners had to step around a huge pile of firewood at the back in order to find seats along the outside edges. The smoke from the generator made the air inside almost impossible to breathe, and there was constant coughing. As an unwritten courtesy, the men took turns sitting at the back, where the air was relatively cleaner.

Flossenburg was more than a hundred miles away, and the lorry could only travel at a maximum speed of twenty miles per hour. It also had to stop every hour in order for the air filters to be cleaned and the generator restoked. During these breaks, the prisoners were able to wander around outside under a loose guard. The weather was glorious, and despite the pounding off to the west, Dietrich could not help but be reminded of his boyhood days in the country at Wangenheimstrasse. The tranquility of nature, even in the midst of the manic destructiveness of war, also reminded him that God, as creator and judge, was not threatened by the paltry activities of one generation of humankind.

In the evenings, the lorry would stop at a village or town and the guards, who by this time were not antagonistic toward the prisoners, would try to find hospitable lodging for the night. This was not easy to do since most townspeople did not trust soldiers. On Monday and Tuesday nights, though, the prisoners found themselves dining on soup and bread and sleeping on scattered blankets.

On Wednesday, they reached the town of Weiden, near Flossenburg. The guards who were driving the lorry suddenly changed their manner toward the prisoners, appearing at the back and ordering them to stay put during the stop. There was tension in their voices.

After a few minutes, several new soldiers were there, one of them holding a clipboard in his gloved hands. He pointed at two prisoners whom Dietrich knew slightly from their connection to the conspiracy. Dietrich leaned back behind his seatmate in order to escape their detection, but even as he was doing this, a friend of one of the two men jumped off the lorry to join them. This seemed to satisfy the soldiers, and they took the three men away, presumably to Flossenburg.

Then the lorry moved down the road again, and a sense of exhilaration swept through the remaining prisoners as they headed south and away from the stench of the death camp. Their good mood was heightened further as the lorry was replaced with a more modern bus that the drivers had been able to requisition outside Weiden.

Late that afternoon the bus reached Schonberg, where the prisoners were put up in an abandoned schoolhouse. The building had large windows that could be opened to let the breezes in from the surrounding valley, and cots with colored blankets were lined up against the walls. There was even an electrical outlet, and the men took turns using Payne Best's electric razor to shave the thick stubble from their faces.

Dietrich spent the next couple of days sitting by an open window and soaking in the springtime sun. Much of the time he was joined by Wasiliew Korokin, the sole Russian in their midst and a nephew of the famous statesman Molotov. Korokin was an atheist, but the two men were overheard discussing the fundamentals of Christianity, and also chess, which was a mutual passion. Once again, Dietrich proved himself capable of becoming friends with just about anybody, under just about any circumstance.

When the morning dawned on the Sunday after Easter, Dietrich was surprised to be asked by the predominantly Catholic group of men to preach a Sunday service. At first he hesitated because he did not want to give his newfound friend, Korokin, the wrong impression. But when even the Russian urged him to go ahead, he assented.

Crisp morning sunlight poured through the tall windows of the small schoolhouse as Dietrich stood and turned in his small Bible to Isaiah 53:5. "And with his stripes we are healed," he read, and then he turned to 1 Peter 1:3: "Blessed be the God and Father of our Lord Jesus Christ, which according to his abundant mercy hath begotten us again unto a lively hope by the resurrection of Jesus Christ from the dead."

Dietrich closed the Bible and spoke about what these verses meant to him.[4] He spoke about how Christ's death truly makes the prisoner free, and how it releases a man from the death that grips his soul because of sin. He spoke about how the resurrection of Christ truly created a new race of men, but not a race of supermen. This new race lived without the clinging stain of the past, and could, by faith, always look forward to a better day, no matter their earthly condition.

The assembled prisoners listened to Dietrich in reverent silence and were touched by his sincerity and by the depth of comfort he himself found in the Scriptures. As a fellow prisoner, he had voiced the feelings that they had all felt at one time or another—the yearnings for freedom, the hopes for a future. Yet he had also provided them with the means by which those desires might be, in their deepest sense, fulfilled.

Before Dietrich could even sit down again, two Gestapo agents in civilian clothes walked into the room and said sternly, "Prisoner Bonhoeffer, get ready and come with us." Everybody instantly knew what this meant. The authorities had finally caught up with him, and there would be no more evasions, no more interrogations. In fact, on Saturday someone in the highest echelons of the Nazi hierarchy (possibly even Hitler himself) had ordered that Dietrich be executed as soon as possible. The order had come down based on "signed" confessions, delivered by the Gestapo agent Keltenbrunner.

As he left with the two men, Dietrich asked Payne Best to tell Bishop Bell what had happened, if he ever got the opportunity. Best nodded, his blue eyes welling up with tears.

That Sunday was spent traveling back to Flossenburg. In the evening, there was a short and formal court martial proceeding, in which the evidence against Dietrich was read aloud and the accused was disallowed from saying anything in his own defense. The sentence was then announced.

At dawn the next morning, Dietrich was taken from his cell and ordered to strip. Before he was taken to the gallows, he was allowed to kneel and pray on the cold concrete floor. Then he was taken outside.

A camp doctor was standing by to confirm Dietrich's death. Later he reported, "In the almost fifty years that I worked as a doctor, I have hardly ever seen a man die so entirely submissive to the will of God."[5]

A few weeks later, World War II ended in Europe.

epilogue

Dietrich Bonhoeffer is best remembered as someone who strove to be a man of God in a time and
place that had no use for him. Yet Bonhoeffer
would not have called himself a man of God. He would
have said, and did say, that he was only a man—nothing
more and nothing less. He was a man who loved God and
tried to serve Him, but he was also a man who made mis-
takes and at times questioned God's purposes.

Preeminently, he was a man who knew that he could
only achieve true manhood by allowing himself to be
inwardly transformed into the image of the incarnate Christ.
And the incarnate Christ took sin and guilt upon Himself in
order to save others. Bonhoeffer believed he was doing close
to the same thing when he became involved in the conspiracy against Hitler's life. He did so fully aware that he might
also suffer the same fate as his Lord.

Certainly Bonhoeffer did not have a death wish, or

even a desire to be a martyr. He deeply enjoyed life and tried to live it to the fullest. He was a skillful musician, a lover of literature, an energetic friend, and one of the most brilliant minds of the century. His daily life was anchored in the simple disciplines of Bible study and prayer, and yet he practiced these disciplines with an intensity that none of his students could duplicate.

After a certain point in his theological training, Bonhoeffer never read the Bible without asking what the Word was telling him to do—right then, right there, wherever he was. Thus the Word took on an immediate and fearsome reality for him. It led him to become the antithesis of what "religious" Germans thought a Christian should be. He had no use for the abstract God of religious observance because such a God had been too easily appropriated by the Nazis. No, he only worshiped the God who had taken on flesh Himself—who had, because of the sins of many, suffered the ultimate punishment before rising again in victory.

For Bonhoeffer, the truth that fulfillment can only be found on the other side of suffering gradually took on a vivid reality. As a lived truth, it became so fully integrated into his life that he was able to say, on the way to his execution, "This is the end—for me, the beginning of life."

Dietrich Bonhoeffer's life can serve as a model for twenty-first-century Christians who are faced with the prospect of newly emerging paganisms and overweening rulers. While the world will never make it convenient for us to be disciples of Christ, Bonhoeffer showed that it is possible to grow in faith through any circumstance, and to be a disciple in any situation or dilemma. He also showed, however, that this could only be done if the disciple was willing to count the cost, and to pay it in full if necessary.

Notes

Prologue
1. Dietrich Bonhoeffer, *Letters and Papers from Prison* (New York: Collier Books, 1971), 21–22.

Chapter 7
1. Eberhard Bethge, *Dietrich Bonhoeffer: Man of Vision, Man of Courage* (New York: Harper & Row, 1970), 194.
2. Geffrey B. Kelly and F. Burton Nelson, eds., *A Testament to Freedom: The Essential Writings of Dietrich Bonhoeffer* (San Francisco Harper: 1990), 205.
3. Ibid., 210.
4. Ibid., 211–12.
5. Bethge, 183.

Chapter 8
1. Bethge, 191.
2. Kelly and Nelson, 139.
3. Ibid., 142–44.

Chapter 9
1. Edwin Robertson. *The Shame and the Sacrifice: The Life and Teaching of Dietrich Bonhoeffer* (London: Hodder & Stoughton, 1987), 107.

Chapter 10
1. Bethge, 263.
2. Quoted in Bethge, 297.
3. Quoted in Bethge, 299.
4. Kelly and Nelson, 430.
5. Ibid., 239–40.
6. Ibid., 443.
7. Ibid., 447.

Chapter 11
1. Kelly and Nelson, 280.

Chapter 12

1. Robertson, 142.
2. Kelly and Nelson, 323–39. Reprinted with the permission of Scribner, a Division of Simon & Schuster, Inc., from *The Cost of Discipleship* by Dietrich Bonhoeffer. Copyright © 1959 by SCM Press Ltd.

Chapter 14

1. Robertson, 171.
2. Quoted in Robertson, 172.
3. Kelly and Nelson, 504.

Chapter 15

1. Kelly and Nelson, 521.
2. Ibid., 523.

Chapter 17

1. Kelly and Nelson, 512. Originally published in "The Other Letters from Prison," *Union Seminary Quarterly Review,* v.23, no. 1 (Fall, 1967), 23–29. Used by permission.
2. Ibid., 513.
3. Ruth-Alice Von Bismarck and Ulrich Kabitz, eds., *Love Letters from Cell 92: The Correspondence Between Dietrich Bonhoeffer and Maria von Wedemeyer, 1943–1945* (London: Harper-Collins, 1984), 96.
4. Bonhoeffer, 32.

Chapter 18

1. Bonhoeffer, 279.
2. Ibid., 280.
3. Ibid., 281.
4. Ibid., 311–12.
5. Ibid., 336–37.

Chapter 19

1. Kelly and Nelson, 380. Reprinted with the permission of Scribner, a Division of Simon & Schuster, Inc., from *Ethics* by Dietrich Bonhoeffer. Copyright © 1955 MacMillan Publishing Co.
2. Ibid., 376.

Chapter 21

1. Kelly and Nelson, 542–43.
2. Ibid., 539–40. Reprinted with the permission of Scribner, a Division of Simon & Scuster, Inc., from *Letters and Papers from Prison* by Dietrich Bonhoeffer. Copyright © 1953, 1967, 1971 by SCM Press Ltd.
3. Quoted in Robertson, 273.
4. Robertson, 275–76.
5. Quoted in Robertson, 277.

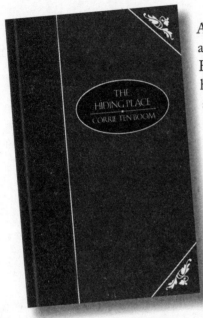